My Wish

Don't Get Swept Away As A Teen

Tantalus Books
Fort Collins, Colorado

Library of Congress Cataloging-in-Publication Data
Boon, Dave.
My wish : don't get swept away as a teen / by Dave Boon.
p. cm.
ISBN 978-0-922530-18-2 (alk. paper)
1. Decision making in adolescence. 2. Teenagers—Conduct of life. I. Title.
BF724.3.D47B66 2008   155.5'1383--dc22
2008011921

Printed in Canada

10 9 8 7 6 5 4 3 2 1

978-0-922530-18-2

Book and Cover design by Twilight Design.

Acknowledgments

My Wish, Dave Boon, Tantalus Books, 2008

You could say this book has been born of floods, storms, and avalanches. I have a continuing *flood* of ideas that I so want my teenage friends to explore. These ideas keep transforming into brain*storms* about speeches and chapter titles. Finally, it took a real *avalanche* to put it all together. I'm convinced that I would only have a flood of unorganized ideas if it weren't for several wonderful people.

To Rick Griggs for believing in me and helping turn my passion for helping kids into a book that will help many others. For your relentless effort of pushing me to get the manuscript completed and for your guidance and mentoring—your friendship will never be forgotten.

Many thanks go to intern/editors like Nicole Davies and April Franklin of Colorado State University's School of Journalism for molding the chapters into readable form. I appreciate the 'sharp eye' of those who did the proofing— Toni Bermudez, Rita Gordon, Karen McManus, Jennifer Peters, Susan Graham, Patty Cromwell, June Boon, Melissa Kelley and Kim Starling.

To Denali, Logan, and Mike you are all the best kids a father could have. I have learned so much from each of you and I am honored and privileged to have you in my life. A special thanks to all the other teens I have gotten to know over the years through tennis, the Boys and Girls Club, Partners of Larimer County, Interact, YRYLA, and schools where I have spoken. Many thanks to all of you for letting me inside your personal world, for sharing your stories with me, and for letting me inspire you through my presentations and stories.

I would like to acknowledge Danny Cox who encouraged me to focus my motivational writing and speaking on an underserved population, our youth! Danny also introduced me to another "uncommon friend" Jim Newton. Thank you both for helping me focus my efforts on our youth with the hope of inspiring them to carry this country to new frontiers with vision, courage, and creativity.

I am especially appreciative of a very special friend and mentor, John Goddard, who's life list first inspired me decades ago. Thank you for your friendship, encouragement, and your willingness to allow me to share your life list with thousands of youth each year. You are such a giving person and one of my heroes!

Finally to my best friend, business associate, and soul mate, my beautiful wife June, who watched, prodded, encouraged, and supported my efforts on this book. You are the love of my life!

Dedication

My Wish is dedicated to Mike Garcia who had a teen journey to hell and back. Your strength and perseverance is an inspiration to us all. To all teens, *My Wish* is dedicated to you with the hope that it will help you stay happy, healthy, and productive on your journey to finding your true purpose in life. That is my wish!

Contents

Preface

Over the past 20 years I have been a high school teacher, a community college and university professor, an Executive Director for the second largest mentoring program in Colorado for "at-risk" youth, a tennis professional, and a life skills coach. In these various positions I have worked with teenagers of all ages and from all social and economic backgrounds. I have seen teenagers that have everything going for them lose sight of a bright future and I have seen teenagers that have been raised in low income single parent families succeed at developing their potential. My wife and I have raised two very successful, happy, and productive children and I have often wondered what makes the difference between a child that loses sight of a bright future and one that stays on track to achieve their dreams. It breaks my heart to see children and teenagers without dreams, without guidance, without the ability to see beyond their current situations. As I have observed and worked with youth over the years I have noticed that successful teenagers have certain character traits and habits. It is my hope that this book contains some wisdom, something that strikes a chord in you to change or reinforce behaviors and patterns of thought that prevent you from overcoming the difficulties that every teenager encounters and those that might be unique to you.

My calling in life is to "save kids' lives." I cannot stand to lose a kid to drugs, alcohol or crime and it hurts me to my very soul to see young people not reach their full potential in life. I used to work with "at risk" youth, but show me a youth that is not at risk in today's world! I prefer to say that I work with children and teens with "unmet potential."

I have only one goal through my presentations at schools, my web site, this book, and my interaction with kids on a daily basis. That goal, my purpose in life, my wish, is to help teens and young adults discover their gifts and their direction in life. I want each and every one of you to become a healthy, happy, and productive member of our world. I don't want you to get "swept away" by drugs, alcohol or negative associations. That is why I wrote this book. That is my purpose—that is my wish!

Chapter 1

Swept Away in an Avalanche!

"I know that this work is ruled by infinite intelligence."
⚭ **Thomas Edison**

Swept Away

I was marveling at the gorgeous sky when something caught my eye about 10 yards ahead and to the left of our car. A small cloud of powder slid down onto the road. Both of my hands were on the steering wheel, and this little white puff of powder was the only warning we got. Less than a second later, our car was literally blown out of control and slammed into the guard rail by a blast of air and snow. It was a total whiteout. I could not see past my windshield, and I could hear snow and ice hitting our car as it was being pummeled by a 120 mph wind. One moment I was going 45 mph looking at royal blue sky, and the next, something very wrong was going on. My mind knew I had not hit another car, and I wasn't in a car accident. I just thought, "What is going on?!"

The next instant, we were hit by an incredible force; it felt like we were hit by a freight train. The impact caused the car to flip into the air, and then I realized what was happening. We had been swept away by an avalanche—a massive avalanche. Everything went dark, as we rolled over and over in total darkness. We must have flipped several times in the air before we hit the ground and started to roll. We had driven this road hundreds, if not a thousand times, and I thought about the steepness of the slope the avalanche was raging down—with us in it! We went for quite a long, wild ride. Everything was black. We just kept rolling. Then we hit something and the car starting spinning upside down. We started slowing down and as we did, June shouted, "Make an air space, make an air space!" The avalanche training we had taken more than 20 years ago flashed back into her mind. Everything was dark. We were upside down, and we were buried alive.

January 6, 2007, had started as a beautiful winter day in Colorado—cold and crystal clear. The sky was deep royal blue, not a cloud in the sky, as my wife June and I made our way up Berthoud Pass on Highway 40. We had picked up 13-year-old Gary Martinez at about 7 a.m. on Saturday, and were heading up for two days of skiing at the Winter Park/ Mary Jane Ski area. We had met Gary at the Boys and Girls Club of Larimer County, Fort Collins Unit. Gary was in the First Serve Fort Collins program that I run at the club, which uses tennis as a platform to teach kids life skills and help them with schoolwork.

Winter Park is our favorite ski area in Colorado for both its family centered atmosphere and its easy access from our home in Fort Collins. Since we have a small cabin there that we own with our dear friend, we usually go up the night before to avoid the morning ski traffic. Another friend of our family was supposed to be going skiing with us, but his work schedule had changed, and he waited until late on Friday night to tell us that he couldn't make it. We didn't realize until later that this may have been more than an unfortunate coincidence.

The trip down Interstate 25 from Fort Collins to Denver was uneventful. Traffic was moving along at a good pace, and we talked about how good the skiing would be that day. There were several large snow storms over the Christmas holiday, and it snowed again just a few days before our trip. The powder promised to be exceptional that weekend.

When we headed west on Interstate 70, the traffic started slowing down, and by the time we reached the Morrison exit, where the Interstate starts climbing steeply into the Rocky Mountains, the traffic had all but come to a stand still. Oh boy! This was going to be a long drive. The traffic did not improve, and it took us nearly 90 minutes to travel 31 miles to the turnoff at Highway 40. We finally got off the interstate at Highway 40 and went through the small town of Empire. We had Gary on the lookout for bighorn sheep since we usually see them between the interstate and Empire. No bighorns this time. We continued to climb toward Berthoud Pass as we pointed out avalanche chutes to Gary. As we rounded the hairpin turn at the Henderson Mine turnoff, I mentioned that we had not seen these avalanches run in quite some time.

We started the steep climb toward the summit of Berthoud Pass, and the song *Affirmation* by Savage Garden started to play on the CD player. Stanley Mountain, rising to a height of 12,524 feet, was on our left as we saw the first "Avalanche

Area—No Stopping" signs. Seconds later and with no warning, the avalanche hit. It blew us up and over the guard rail and rolled us over and over. We hit the tree and came to a stop upside down—buried alive.

Digging Out

My side window blew in on me when the avalanche hit. I stuck my hand out, and when I pulled it back, I could see daylight. I immediately asked June, "Are you OK? Are you with me?" She replied, "Yes." I asked Gary, "Are you OK? Are you with me?" He also replied, "Yes." Then I said, "We're going to be OK. We've got air!" It took me several minutes to get my seatbelt released. All the snow inside our car—and there was a lot—had jammed the release mechanism, making it difficult to unbuckle. Finally it released, and I dug my way out through my side window.

I immediately turned around and went back into the car head first to dig the snow away from June's face. She was spitting snow and crumbs of glass. Her head was in a low position in the car, so all the snow that was still sifting in was piling up around her head. I dug like crazy to get the snow away so she could breathe. Once I had her face cleared, I tried to release her seatbelt. Hers was even tighter than mine. It wouldn't come loose!

I crawled back out through my glassless window and stood up. I could see people standing way above us on Highway 40 looking down, and a few people had started down the slope with shovels. I couldn't see clearly because my glasses had been blown off my face when the avalanche hit us. I screamed at the top of my lungs, "Call 911 and somebody get me a knife. Get me a knife now!" I dropped to my knees and went back inside the car. More snow had accumulated around June's face, so I helped her clear it again. She was starting to breathe harder and faster, but I couldn't do anything to free her until someone brought me a knife.

I turned my attention to Gary in the backseat. I said to Gary, "It's time to get you out." Gary was able to snake his way between the two front seats and out my window. He was bleeding a little from a cut on his face, but he looked OK, although he was a little shaken up. After all, we had just been hit by a massive avalanche, thrown down a steep slope, broken a tree, and been buried alive. I asked him if he was OK, and he replied, "Yes."

I went back inside the car to check on June. She was starting to panic a bit. As I crawled in through the window I heard her say, "Calm down. I need to calm down." I cleared some snow from her face again and held her hand. She told me she was very uncomfortable and that her head, which was pinned between the collapsed roof and her head rest, was starting to really hurt. Gravity was pushing her down and lodging her head tighter. I held her hand and reassured her that everything was going to be alright. Someone would come any minute with a knife, and we would get her out. It had been more than 10 minutes since we were hit and buried, and she was pinned upside down with her head trapped the entire time.

Finally, I heard someone say that he had a knife. I came back out the window and told the guy to wait a minute—I never got your name, so thank you. Someone had found my avalanche shovel that was thrown from our trunk when we hit the tree. He had been digging out the driver side of the car. I took the shovel and shattered the only intact window, the driver side back window, and crawled into the backseat. I pushed up on June's head and shoulders while the man cut her shoulder restrain. She was pulled out the side window and was finally free!

I crawled out from the backseat. As I stood up, June pointed to the van that had ended up about 100 feet below us. I turned and got a sick feeling in my stomach, and I thought, "I hope they are OK." June immediately told the people who helped us, "We're OK. Go check on them. They are probably in worse shape than we are." Everyone who had gathered around our car started running toward the other car to help. We were left completely alone. We turned to each other and had a big group hug. At that exact moment, the CD player started playing right where it had left off when the avalanche hit us—*Affirmation* by Savage Garden.

Alive and Well

I had blood seeping down the left side of my face from several small cuts on my head. My left hand was bleeding from some small cuts, and I had blood coming out of my mouth from where I had chomped into my tongue. My back hurt, June's right shoulder hurt, and Gary said his jaw hurt. All in all, we were OK, just a little banged up. We found out later that we had no serious injuries, and we were very fortunate to be alive. We looked up at the road. It seemed so far away and so steep. Then I noticed the tree that we had hit. It was 10 to12 inches in diameter and was lying right next to the other side of the car pointing downhill. It took us about 10 minutes to climb the hill and get back to the road. When we finally reached the road, we were on the east side of the avalanche-debris-field and had to climb up and over it—WOW! It was a really big pile of snow. We learned later from the Colorado Department of Transportation that it was 18 feet deep.

We were so cold and shivering uncontrollably. I was only wearing a long sleeve tee-shirt, and my pants were soaked from the waist down from standing in the snow. June was wearing her coat. I had pulled my coat out from the backseat before we headed up the hill and put it around Gary. Even with their coats on, they were shivering uncontrollably. Someone offered me a coat, and then I asked if I could borrow a cell phone to call Gary's mother and my daughters to tell them we were OK. We went by ambulance to St. Anthony's Hospital in Denver, Colorado. We were released around 3:35 p.m. We learned that four of five passengers in the van from Iowa had also walked out of the accident, and only one had to spend the night in the hospital. He was released the next day.

Lessons Learned from Being Swept Away

- We are more grateful for all the family and friends that we have in our lives. So be grateful.
- We are highly energized to do more of what we feel we should be doing in this world. Get energized.
- We have always believed that people are inherently good, and this experience has renewed that faith in us because of all the

individuals who helped out at the avalanche site. Have faith in people.

- We don't dwell on the little things because they are unimportant in the grand scheme of things. Focus on life.

- We see more humor in life and laugh at things and situations that may have bothered us before the accident. Keep a smile on your face.

- We believe in divine intervention and truly value our lives. Believe in miracles!

Believe in Miracles—They Do Happen

Whether you believe in miracles or divine intervention; whether you believe in God, Buddha, Allah, Jehovah, or something else, I must tell you that something or someone intervened that day to protect all eight of the individuals that were hit by the massive avalanche. I was speaking to a dear friend shortly after the accident about what had happened and asked her thoughts on God, Allah, Buddha, and Jehovah and whether she thought any one of them had anything to do with our miracle survival. She replied, "Yes—I think it must have been a team effort." I guess that someone has a bigger plan for me and that I must still have lots of work to do on this planet.

I want each and every one of you to become a healthy, happy, and productive member of our world. I don't want you to get "swept away" by drugs, alcohol or negative associations. That is why I wrote this book. That is my purpose—that is my wish!

Getting It Done!

- Be grateful for your life on this planet. Make a list of the things you are grateful for. Start with the basic necessities like being grateful for food, clean water, sanitation, a roof over your head, and free education. You can build on this list and include things like family, friends, pets, beautiful sunrises and sunsets, music, movies, hospitals, cars, highways, and airplanes. It's your list of grateful things. Make sure you list at least fifty things!

- Make a personal vow to "discover your gift," your special purpose in life.

- Follow the steps outlined in this book to help you on your journey through the turbulent teenage years.

  1. Have dreams and goals.

  2. Take action through personal initiative.

  3. Find people, we'll call them mentors, to help you on your journey.

  4. Promise yourself that you will never, never, never give up!

Chapter 2

Show the World: Dreams Do Come True

"Would you help me please," Alice asked, "which way ought I to go from here?" "That depends a good deal on where you want to get to," said the Cat. "I don't much care where," said Alice. "Then it doesn't matter which way you go," said the Cat.
༄ *Alice in Wonderland*, **Lewis Carroll**

It's Christmas Eve—Dream

Can you remember a time in your life when you were so excited you couldn't go to sleep? Not a time when you were so stressed out about a test or event that you were restless but a time when you were filled with positive excitement. So much excitement that you couldn't go to sleep or you woke up early the next morning? When I ask teens this question, the two most common memories of this type of excitement are traveling (often to another country) and experiencing Christmas Eve as young children. What would life be like if this was how it was each and every day? It would be a very exciting time, even if it is a little sleep deprived. Being sleep deprived is nothing new for teens but feeling excited about what you're doing, what you're planning to see, and what you're going to achieve is uncommon for teens.

At one time, these were some of my dreams: go on an archaeological expedition in the second largest desert in the world—I was only 15 when I did this—learn to fly, own an airplane, learn to scuba dive, surf Rincon, Puerto Rico, raft the Yampa/Green River through Dinosaur National Park, learn to ice climb, go to college on both an athletic and academic scholarship, travel to Krakow, Poland and visit Auschwitz Concentration Camp. I also wanted to visit the Jagelonian University and see Copernicus' thesis of the universe, walk across the Charles Bridge in Prague, run a non-profit organization that helps kids, teach tennis for the number one player in the world, help 20 colleges start environmental programs, visit our nation's capitol in Washington, D.C., start a First Serve program, teach kid's tennis so they can get a full-ride college scholarship, coach a national champion, and help my niece beat her methamphetamine *(meth)* addiction. These are just a few of the dreams that I have already achieved, but how did it happen? How do you go about dreaming dreams and finding the time, skill, and money to make them come true?

> *"Just because a man lacks the use of his eyes doesn't mean he lacks vision."*
> ∞ **Stevie Wonder**

It All Starts with Vision

If you play a sport, then your coaches have probably introduced you to a tool called "visual imagery." Visual imagery is the ability to see yourself, with your mind, not your eyes, achieving some feat. It could be making a free throw, breaking the tape at the finish line, serving an ace, making a perfect header on a corner kick, or knocking the ball out of the park. Visual imagery has been proven time and time again to be a very powerful tool for helping you to believe in your dreams and goals and to ultimately achieve them. Every top athlete uses this technique, but it can be used in every part of your life. This is the first step toward achieving great things. Some call it the "power of attraction." Regardless of what you call it, it works!

John Goddard—A Teen with a Vision

I finally had the pleasure of meeting John Goddard in November of 2005 when he gave a presentation in Fort Collins, Colorado. I had read about this amazing man when I was young and always wanted to meet him. He inspired me at a young age to want to travel and explore the world around me. He wrote about his travels and adventures and had them published in *Life, National Geographic,* and *Chicken Soup for the Soul* as well as in his book, *The Survivor: 24 Spine-Chilling Adventures on the Edge of Death.*

How would you like to climb the highest mountain on a continent, fly at the speed of sound, land and take off from an aircraft carrier? Would you like to explore the ocean in a submarine, run a five minute mile, parachute from a plane, or play classical music on the piano? How about write a book, raft the Grand Canyon, kayak the world's longest river, visit the Galapagos Islands, become an Eagle Scout, or circumnavigate the globe—John has four times. John did all of these things and much more.

When John was 15-years-old, he overheard his father having a discussion with a friend. His father's friend said, "If I was John's age, I would do things a lot differently." As adults, we call those regrets—I wish I had done that, I should have done that, or I could have done that. John didn't want to live a life of regrets. He took out a yellow legal pad of paper and wrote across the top, "My Life List." He then proceeded to write down 127 things that he wanted to see, do, and be in life.

John Goddard was the first man to explore the entire length of the world's longest river, the Nile, in a 4,160 mile expedition that took nine months. The *Los Angeles Times* called his voyage "the most amazing adventure of this generation." He then matched that achievement and became the first man to explore the entire length of another African river, the Congo. He established numerous records as a civilian jet pilot, including a speed record of 1,500 mph in the F-111 Fighter-Bomber, and an altitude record of 63,000 feet in the F-106 Delta Dart.

John graduated from the University of Southern California with a bachelor's degree in anthropology and psychology. He has studied obscure cultures in all parts of the globe. In addition, he has climbed 12 of the world's tallest mountains, conducted 14 major expeditions into remote regions, traversed 15 of the world's most treacherous rivers, visited 120 countries, studied 260 primitive tribes, and traveled more than one million miles during his adventurous life.

Honored by the U.S. Junior Chamber of Commerce as one of California's outstanding young men, John belongs to the Adventurers' Club of Los Angeles and was the youngest member ever admitted. He is also a member of the Adventurers' Club of Chicago, the Explorers' Club of New York, the Savage Club of London, the Royal Geographic Society, the French Explorers' Society as the only American member, the Archaeological Society, the Mach II Club, and the Sigma Chi Fraternity, of which he is a life member.

John, who lives with his wife in southern California, does not believe in pursuing adventure for the sake of frivolous thrills, but used these experiences to achieve a worthwhile end. This end, for him, is scientific exploration and adding to the world's store of knowledge. "Digging out the facts is the real challenge," John said of his life. "The adventure is exciting and enjoyable, but secondary."

Yet, digging out the facts can be a hazardous occupation. John has been bitten by a rattlesnake, charged by an elephant, and trapped in quicksand. He has been in plane crashes, caught in earthquakes, and almost drowned twice while running rapids. But his overwhelming desire to discover fresh knowledge and to complete his youthful list of goals has driven him on in spite of the danger.

Today, he has accomplished 114 of the original 127 goals that he listed the day he drafted his "My Life List." The thirteen goals that he has not yet achieved are marked with an astric (*). John Goddard is the most amazing person I have ever met and is walking proof that dreams do come true if you have a vision of where you want to go, a written list of your dreams and goals, take action in achieving those dreams and goals, find people to help you on your journey, and decide to never give up. You too, can have an amazing life of achievements just like John. Let's take a look at the list that John wrote at 15-years-old, when he decided to show the world that dreams do come true.

My Life List, By John Goddard

Explore:

1. Nile River, Africa
2. Amazon River, South America
3. Congo River, Africa
4. Colorado River, North America
5. Yangtze River, China
*6. Niger River, Africa
*7. Orinoco River, Venezuela
8. Rio Coco, Nicaragua

Study Native Cultures In:

9. Congo
10. New Guinea
11. Brazil
12. Borneo
13. Sudan
14. Australia
15. Kenya
16. The Philippines
17. Tanganyika *(now Tanzania)*
18. Ethiopia
19. Nigeria
20. Alaska

Climb:

*21. Mount Everest, Nepal

*22. Mount Aconcagua, Argentina

*23. Mount McKinley, U.S.A.

24. Mount Huascaran, Peru

25. Mount Kilimanjaro, Africa

26. Mount Ararat, Turkey

27. Mount Kenya, Kenya

*28. Mount Cook, New Zealand

29. Mount Popocatepetl, Mexico

30. The Matterhorn, Switzerland

31. Mount Rainer, U.S.A.

32. Mount Fuji, Japan

33. Mount Vesuvius, Italy

34. Mount Bromo, Indonesia

35. Grand Tetons, U.S.A.

36. Mount Baldy, U.S.A.

Study and Learn:

37. Carry out careers in medicine and exploration

*38. Visit every country in the world *(30 to go)*

39. Study Navaho and Hopi Indians

40. Learn to fly a plane

41. Ride a horse in a Rose Bowl Parade

Photograph:

42. Iguaçu Falls, Brazil
43. Victoria Falls, Rhodesia
44. Sutherland Falls, New Zealand
45. Yosemite Falls, U.S.A.
46. Niagara Falls, Canada/U.S.A.
47. Retrace the travels of Marco Polo and Alexander the Great

Explore Underwater:

48. Coral Reef, U.S.A.
49. Great Barrier Reef, Australia
50. Red Sea, Africa/Asia
51. Fiji Islands, Oceania
52. The Bahamas, Caribbean
53. Explore Okefenokee and Everglades, U.S.A.

Visit:

*54. North and South Poles, Canada and Antarctica
55. Great Wall of China, China
56. Panama & Suez Canals, Panama and Egypt
57. Easter Island, Chile
58. The Galapagos Islands, Ecuador
59. Vatican City, Apennine Peninsula
60. The Taj Mahal, India
61. The Eiffel Tower, France
62. The Blue Grotto, Italy

63. The Tower of London, U.K. of Great Britain

64. The Leaning Tower of Pisa, Italy

65. Sacred Well of Chichen-Itza, Mexico

66. Climb Ayers Rock, Australia

67. Follow River Jordon from Sea of Galilee to the Dead Sea, Asia

Swim In:

68. Lake Victoria, Africa

69. Lake Superior, U.S.A./Canada

70. Lake Tanganyika, Tanzania

71. Lake Titicaca, Peru

72. Lake Nicaragua, Nicaragua

Accomplish:

73. Become an Eagle Scout

74. Dive in a submarine

75. Land on and take off from an aircraft carrier

76. Fly in a blimp, hot air balloon, and glider

77. Ride an elephant, camel, ostrich and bronco

78. Skin dive to 40 feet, hold breath for 2½ minutes

79. Catch a 10 pound lobster and 10 inch abalone

80. Play a flute and violin

81. Type 50 words a minute

82. Take a parachute jump

83. Learn water and snow skiing

84. Go on a church mission

85. Follow the John Muir Trail

86. Study native medicines, bring back useful ones

87. Bag camera trophies of elephant, lion, rhino, cheetah, Cape buffalo, and whale

88. Learn to fence

89. Learn jujitsu

90. Teach a college course

91. Watch a cremation ceremony in Bali

92. Explore the depths of the sea

*93. Appear in a Tarzan movie

*94. Own a horse, chimp, cheetah, ocelot, and coyote *(Chimp and cheetah to go)*

*95. Become a ham radio operator

96. Build own telescope

97. Write a book

98. Publish article in *National Geographic*

99. High jump 5 feet

100. Broad jump 15 feet

101. Run a mile in five minutes

102. Weigh 175 pounds *(still does)*

103. Perform 200 sit-ups and 20 push-ups

104. Learn French, Spanish, and Arabic

105. Study dragon lizards of Komodo Island

106. Visit birthplace of Grandfather Sorrenson

107. Visit birthplace of Grandfather Goddard

108. Ship aboard a freighter as a seaman

*109. Read the entire Encyclopedia Britannica

110. Read the Bible cover to cover

111. Read the works of Shakespeare, Plato, Aristotle, Thoreau, Poe, Rousseau, Bacon, Hemingway, Dickens, Twain, Burroughs, Conrad, Talmage, Tolstoy, Longfellow, Keats, Whittier, and Emerson

112. Become familiar with the compositions of Bach, Beethoven, Debussy, Ibert, Mendelssohn, Lalo, Rimsky-Korsakov, Respighi, Liszt, Rachmaninoff, Stravinsky, Toch, Tchaikovsky, and Verdi

113. Become proficient in the use of a plane, motorcycle, tractor, surfboard, rifle, pistol, canoe, microscope, football, basketball, bow and arrow, lariat, and boomerang

114. Compose music

115. Play Clair de Lune on the piano

116. Watch fire-walking ceremony in Bali

117. Milk a poisonous snake

118. Light a match with a .22 rifle

119. Visit a movie studio

120. Climb Cheops' Pyramid

121. Become a member of the Explorers' Club and the Adventurers' Club

122. Learn to play polo

123. Travel the Grand Canyon *(by foot and boat)*

124. Circumnavigate the globe *(4 times)*

*125. Visit the moon

126. Marry and have children *(has 5 kids)*

127. Live to see the 21st Century

Your Life List

Time to do what John did and create a life list. Except this one will be *"Your Life List."* Go someplace where you will not be disturbed, turn off your cell phone, and, if you're at your computer, turn off your instant messenger. Take out a piece of paper, and across the top write, *"My Life List,"* in big, bold letters. Now, start writing and don't stop. You can look back at John's list to get some ideas.

List all the things that you want to see. Do you want to visit all the great art museums of the world, look the *Mona Lisa* in the eye, see Michelangelo's *David*, visit our nation's capitol, or visit all the states in the United States? See the Vatican, the Coliseum in Rome, the Great Wall of China, an NFL Super Bowl, an NBA Championship Series, a Stanley Cup Final, a World Series Game, a World Cup soccer match, a concert by a famous musician, or watch a famous artist paint? I don't know what you want to see, just get busy writing down all the things that you can think of.

List the things you want to do. Where would you like to travel in the world? Italy, Spain, France, Petra, the Holy Land, Brazil, the Galapagos Islands, Eiffel Tower, Taj Mahal, or Antarctica? Do you want to learn how to scuba dive, sky dive, fly a plane, sail, snowboard, bungee jump, write a book? How about travel the Grand Canyon by raft, visit the moon, or go into outer space? I don't know what you want to do, just get busy! Write down everything that you can think of no matter how impossible it seems. Remember you can always come back and add to the list later as ideas come to you. Over his life, John Goddard's Life List has grown from the original 127 to over 600 and he has accomplished well over 500 of these goals. See, dreams do come true.

Getting It Done!

- Look at your "Life List" daily. Add things to it as you think of them. After creating your "Life List," take action through personal initiative, find mentors to help you achieve these goals, and persevere by never, never, never giving up.

- Put your "My Life List" in a place that you will see it every day. On the mirror of your bathroom, on your wall above your desk, maybe above your bed. Carry an extra copy with you in your notebook. Look at it often and add to it when you hear or see something that triggers the thought, "That would be cool to do. I want to do or see that too."

- Then, take action toward your goals and find people to help you along that path toward achieving your dreams.

- John Goddard would end this discussion this way. "This conversation is to be continued."

Chapter 3

The Power of Associations: Your Peers and Friends—The Good and the Bad Ones

"If you dress like Halloween, ghouls will try to get in your pants."
∞ **John Travolta as Caster Troy in *Face Off***

My Friend Mike

When I first met my friend Mike, he was a sixth-grader attending Laurel Elementary School in Fort Collins, Colorado. I was the executive director of Partners of Larimer County, the second largest mentoring program in Colorado for "at-risk" youth. Mike was in the Partners program and I was matched as his "senior partner," a term given to the adult in the mentoring relationship.

Mike's grandmother had gotten him into the Partners program because he didn't have an active father or a positive adult male role model in his life. Mike was what people often called, "at-risk"—at risk for failure since he was the kid of a single mother and was living in her household, which was considered "poverty level." He was often put in a position of being around drugs and alcohol and seeing his mother being physically abused by boyfriends or ex-husbands. Drugs were often sold out of his mother's home, however, not at his grandmother's home. In addition, no one in his family had ever gone to college, and he was a Latino minority. So you see, Mike really had a number of things going on in his life that were going to make it hard for him to succeed, even though he was bright and very athletic.

I really don't like the label of "at-risk" because I believe that all youth are at risk today—at risk for drugs, teen pregnancy, HIV, school dropout, and other peer pressures that teens must often face on a day-to-day basis. I would prefer the term, "youth with unmet potential" since I want all youth to succeed, and all of you have challenges in your life, regardless of your ethnic background, economic status, or whether you live with both parents or with one. Life is often tough for all youth today, and Mike was no exception.

At 15, he and his mother were taken hostage by her abusive ex-husband who was not Mike's father. The SWAT Team was called, and Mike was lucky enough to get out and escape, but before the ordeal was over, Mike's mother was shot and killed, and then the shooter turned the gun on himself. This was the summer between his freshman and sophomore years in high school. Life became unbelievably tough for Mike after the ordeal, and got even harder for him when he lost his way and started hanging out with bad people who didn't care about him and encouraged him to make poor choices.

I wonder how many people told Mike that he could be really good someday—in football, baseball, or even skiing. Positive encouragement makes all the difference in life, so why was Mike only hearing the people who had a very negative influence on him? I just didn't understand. I was disappointed in Mike, but I was angry, so angry, with whoever was filling his mind with crap.

Mike's Friends

When Mike was doing well in school and playing sports, he had lots of positive support from both his peers and adults. People would go out of their way to tell him what a great game he had played or how proud they were of him for his good work in school.

When Mike was on the streets, he had other types of peers and friends. His peers became his family, and he was tight with them. But to become part of their group and be accepted by them, he had to do what they did. Even though Mike knew that many of the things his friends did were ethically wrong and some were illegal, he still did them because he believed that he needed these friends and that they were more important than staying within the boundaries of the law.

The power of association and acceptance into negative groups or even gangs is often a more powerful pull than associating with a positive group and doing what you know is right and lawful. Why? Peer pressure is a powerful thing and people associating with negative groups will use it to bring others down to their level. It is this power of association and wanting to be part of a group, to be liked, to be accepted, that is the strongest pull that teenagers have to deal with today. Whether it's belonging to a good group or bad group, it's still belonging.

The Four-Way Test

I never really understood why teens feel such a strong need to have friends, good or bad, until I helped conduct a Four-Way Test at Cache la Poudre Junior High School. The Four-Way Test is a Rotary creed, a way to live your life by the highest standards. Rotarians worldwide try to lead their lives by this creed. Here is the Four-Way Test:

The Four-Way Test of things we think, say, or do.

Is it the TRUTH?

Is it FAIR to all concerned?

Will it build GOODWILL and BETTER FRIENDSHIPS?

Will it be BENEFICIAL to all concerned?

At Cache la Poudre Junior High, we asked teens specific questions about unethical things (cheating, lying, stealing, drugs, etc.) and asked what their reaction or response would be in such theoretical situations. I was stunned—no, I was BLOWN AWAY—by how far teens would go to cover for their friends. They would lie, help their friends cheat, cover for them, and not go to an adult to get help when they needed it. They would even cover for friends if they had committed a crime—a serious crime.

You should take a minute when you are about to say something that either isn't true, or will hurt someone, and ask yourself, "Would this pass the Four-Way Test? If the answer is no, don't do it or allow someone else to do it.

Everyone has a choice. The choice you have is whether you want to have positive friendships or negative ones. The choice is yours.

True Friendship

I can count my true friends on one hand, or maybe two hands now that I am older and choosing to hang out with positive people—people who help others, people who care about everyone and not just a select few, people who want to make a positive difference in others. These are some of the attributes of my true friends. Out of the 10 to 20 true friends I have, which is a lot by any standards, only one, whom I haven't seen in approximately 10 years, is from my high school days. WOW! Now think about that. Will the people who you think are very close to you and are your "best friends" still be there when you are in college, out of college, and out on your own? I hope they are, but I am willing to bet that they will not be there for you when times get tough in the future. In fact, they may not be there for you when the times get tough over the next few years.

You have probably seen or been part of a situation wherein someone was popular one day and cast out the next. Most so-called friendships are anything but—they are peers or acquaintances, and your association with them and theirs with you is not often based on true friendship but rather on things that really don't count, such as looks, money, and clothing.

"A friend is one who walks in when the rest of the world walks out."
∞ **Walter Winchell**

What Do You Really Want?

What do you really want and need from your peers and friends? Refer to the chapter entitled, "Leadership: It's Not Just for Adults," and take a look at the list of character traits provided by students in leadership retreats. Which of these do you want in your friends?

Trustworthy—If someone lies about something or talks about people behind their backs, they will do the same thing to you. Why hang out with people you can't trust?

Fair—Do they treat everyone the same—always positive and good? If not, why do you hang around with them? Don't you think it is right to treat everyone fairly?

Respectful—Everyone, and I mean everyone, deserves to be treated with respect. This is one character trait that I often observe is lacking in youth. Are the people you hang out with respectful to everyone? If they don't treat others with respect, why do you hang with them?

Positive Inspiration—Do the people you hang around with pump you up in a positive way? Do they encourage you to go for dreams and goals? Do they have goals and dreams? If they are always negative and discouraging, why would you hang with them?

Responsible—Do they follow through with what they say they are going to do? If they're irresponsible and not dependable, why do you hang out with them?

Integrity—A young nine year old boy, Patrick Cooklin, taught me a great definition of integrity one day. He defined it as doing the right thing when no one is watching you. Do the people you hang with act with integrity? If not, why do you hang with them?

There are many other traits I would like to see in my friends, and I am sure you do too. I want my friends to also be empathetic, caring, loyal, patient, good listeners, and supportive. However, if they are not respectful, trustworthy, inspiring, or a person of integrity, then I must look for other friends.

Random Acts of Kindness or Random Acts of Meanness: For Girls Only

Girls can be so mean! Sometime around middle school or junior high and well into high school, many girls become mean, backstabbing, vicious manipulators. I have seen it firsthand. I have raised two very happy, healthy, and productive daughters, and although they may have played a part in social bullying—we all have at some time—my oldest was the recipient of this type of harassment, and my youngest learned a valuable lesson from watching what happened to her older sister. Sometime between junior high and early high school the group that Denali, our oldest daughter, had always hung out with since elementary school started to change. She wanted to be like and liked by her friends and needed to have the same shoes, clothes, and personal "things" to be accepted by them. If she didn't, she would be ridiculed, made fun of, called names, and might even be kicked out of the popular clique. All of these things happened, and she was miserable.

"I've learned that people will forget what you said, people will forget what you did, but people will never forget how you made them feel."

∞ **Maya Angelou**

I remember in her senior year of high school that Denali couldn't wait to go to college and meet new friends. You see, most of you have friends you have gone to school with since elementary school, and you're tight! But as you reach junior high and high school, you start maturing and making decisions on your own about the type of people you want to be around. Hopefully, those decisions are based on the kind of people they are and what kind of values they have and not on superficial characteristics. We are so proud of Denali and the soul mate she has found, to spend the rest of her life with. I truly believe that many of her old friends will go through divorce and unhappiness in their adult lives because they never stopped the deceitful, backstabbing habits that they learned as teens.

My youngest daughter, Logan, had the opportunity to learn from her older sister's struggles. Logan never talked trash about others and often stood up to people who did and encouraged them to change their ways. And even if she didn't say anything, she still chose not to participate. Logan has always been a person of integrity—both of my daughters are—but one event convinced me that Logan has surpassed her peers in this regard.

We were coming back from a soccer game and her team had lost. I knew Logan did not regard one of the other players on her team in high esteem. In fact, I knew that my daughter didn't even respect her, although Logan always treated her with respect. This teammate often talked trash about other players and often left the team a player short because she didn't always show up. She played to "get even" with players if they beat her on the field, which often cost the team a foul or worse. On this occasion, I felt that this player had actually cost our team the game. She was slow, maybe tired, and had been outplayed several times by an offensive player on the opposing team. She had committed several fouls, and even pulled a player on the other team to the ground and purposely tripped her. One of these fouls led to a penalty kick, which the opposing team scored on and won the game by.

We were in the car heading home after the game, and Logan never took losing easily. I was talking about how I thought this player had cost us the game with her "dirty play." Logan stopped me in my tracks and said, "Dad, I really don't appreciate you talking about one of my teammates like that. Please stop!" She was defending a person whom I knew she did not respect; one she knew had been a part of the negative outcome of the game. She was always kind to that person and respectful, but she would never have picked her as a close friend. And yet, she was doing something very important for this person. She wasn't letting anyone, including her father, put her down.

"Life's most persistent and urgent question is, 'What are you doing for others?'"
∽ **Martin Luther King, Jr.**

Kind Words and Kind Deeds

Here is a great poem by Henry Wadsworth Longfellow that puts the need for positive words and deeds in beautiful verse. It is worth reading each time you find yourself drifting from being a person of integrity.

> *Kind hearts are the gardens,*
> *Kind thoughts are the roots,*
> *Kind words are the flowers,*
> *Kind deeds are the fruits.*
>
> *Take care of your garden*
> *And keep out the weeds,*
> *Fill it with sunshine*
> *Kind words and kind deeds.*

by Henry Wadsworth Longfellow

"If someone were to pay you 10 cents for every kind word you ever spoke and collect five cents for every unkind word, would you be rich or poor?"
∞ **Nonpareil**

Getting It Done!

- Everyone has a choice. Make it a choice to be kind to all and to pick the positive paths in life to get you toward your goals and dreams.

- Be a friend that is trustworthy, fair, respectful, positive, responsible, and always has integrity.

- Pick friends that are trustworthy, fair, respectful, positive, responsible, and always have integrity.

- Apply the Rotary Four-Way Test to the things that you think, say or do.

- Take care of your garden and keep the weeds out.

Chapter 4

Choices: They're All Up to You

"Look for your choices, pick the best one, then go with it."
∞ **Pat Riley**

It Happened One Friday Night

Amanda was a friend of Denali's, and they both played on the Rocky Mountain High School (RMHS) Varsity Soccer Team. It was a Friday night, and Denali had gone out to a party. Amanda was also at the party with some of her friends. We found out later it was a kegger with lots of beer for everyone.

Denali and her boyfriend came home when the party moved from one location to another. They had not been drinking, and after getting something to eat, they settled in for a movie.

After Denali left the party, Amanda made the choice to follow the party and climbed into the back of an open-top Jeep. There wasn't enough room for everyone, so Amanda went without a seatbelt. The driver had been drinking, and there were too many people in the car. Also leaving the party at about the same time was Chris and his girlfriend, both friends of Denali and Amanda. Chris was a great soccer player and on the boys' RMHS Varsity Soccer Team, and had a state championship playoff game the next day. Chris wasn't drinking, and he was ready for the big game. Chris had recently signed a Letter of Intent with Drexel University and had secured a full-ride scholarship. Things were going very well for both Amanda and Chris.

On the way to the next party, things got out of hand. Chris stopped at a stop sign and was starting to accelerate, when the Jeep Amanda was in ran through the stop sign and broadsided Chris' car. The Jeep spun around, and Amanda was thrown from the car, smashing to the ground and rolling over and over. All of the other passengers took off and left the scene of the accident. The only ones left were the two drivers and Amanda, who was lying unconscious and bleeding on the side of the road. Chris was a good friend of Amanda's, but as he held the bleeding unconscious girl while they waited for the ambulance to arrive, he didn't realize that it was her.

Later that night, a call came in and Denali took off saying that there had been an accident and she had to go to the Emergency Room at our local hospital. Amanda was rushed to the Poudre Valley Hospital and spent three days in intensive care because she had multiple injuries.

Most of Amanda's friends didn't sleep that night, including Chris and Denali. Many stayed at the hospital, and others retreated to their homes, wondering why it had to happen to Amanda. The other passengers just went home and tried to get to their rooms without their parents noticing the beer on their breath.

Having hardly slept, Chris arrived at the soccer game the next day with the accident still on his mind. Chris played defense, but his team got behind early. Shortly after the first goal, the other team was in scoring range again and took a shot. Chris had a chance to block the shot and stuck out his leg, but the ball deflected off his leg and into the goal. He had inadvertently scored on his own team. The stress of the accident the night before, the lack of sleep, and now, accidentally hurting his own team was too much for him to bear. He started to cry. He walked to the side of the field, took off his jersey, dropped it by the sidelines, and walked away. He gave up his scholarship, didn't attend Drexel, and never played competitive soccer again.

Let's take a quick look at some national statistics from past years on teen drivers.

1. Motor vehicle crashes are the leading cause of death for teenagers.

2. 16-year-olds have higher crash rates than drivers of any other age.

3. On average, 25% of teen drivers killed in auto accidents have a blood alcohol concentration (BAC) of .08 or greater. All 50 states define driving with a BAC of .08 or greater as "drunk driving."

4. On average, two-thirds of teens killed in auto accidents each year were not wearing seatbelts.

5. Almost half of the crash deaths involving 16-year-old drivers occur when the beginning drivers were driving with teen passengers.

6. Statistics show that 16- and 17-year-old driver death rates increase with each additional passenger.

Lots of choices were made that night, and many people paid the price for making bad choices. Let's take a look at some of the choices that were made. First of all, the driver of the Jeep chose to drink. Drinking and driving is a very bad decision and is extremely dangerous. No one thinks anything will happen to them, until they get caught, seriously injure someone, or even kill an innocent person. Secondly, everyone who got into the Jeep made a choice to ride with someone that had been drinking—another very bad choice. Thirdly, Amanda was not wearing a seatbelt—a bad choice. Finally, all the passengers were teenagers, and the car had more passengers than the car could safely seat, greatly increasing their chances of having a fatal accident. The only statistic that was not proven true in this situation, thank goodness, was that there were no deaths caused by the accident. Let me restate an important fact.

Motor vehicle crashes are the leading cause of death for teenagers. Don't let your choices make you one of these statistics!

"My best friend is the one who brings out the best in me."
∞ **Henry Ford**

Draw a Line in the Sand

It was early 2001, and I had just been hired as the executive director at Partners of Larimer County. At the time, Partners was the second largest mentoring program in Colorado for "at-risk" youth. I was really excited about this new adventure in my life. I would be helping match adults with youth who needed an adult friend in their lives. What I didn't know was how hard I was going to have to work to raise the roughly $40,000 needed each month to run the organization. Partners had offices in Fort Collins, Loveland, and Estes Park with eight employees. Our goal was to match 100 youth, Junior Partners, each year with 100 caring adult mentors, Senior Partners. I was really excited about taking over the leadership position for this great organization because I think that every young person needs a mentor in their life to help them on the road to success. What I didn't know was that the organization would face financial challenges in just a few short months.

By the summer of 2001, Partners was facing a number of challenges, but it was nothing catastrophic and nothing I couldn't handle. The building we had occupied for a number of years was being sold, and we needed to find a new home. I did not want to rent again and had convinced the board to look for a property we could buy. In addition, our income was declining, and a quick evaluation showed that at the end of any given month we had approximately $14,000 in unrestricted cash in our checking account. Now that might seem like a lot of money, but our monthly payroll alone was approximately $25,000, meaning that I had two to three weeks before we would be out of money unless I could raise the balance.

Then the bottom fell out. The state economy was going down, and our contracts with the state were cancelled, even though we had two to three years left on the contracts and grants. The fine print, however, stated that the funds were only available based on the availability of the funding, meaning that the state could cut these much needed services at any time, and that is exactly what happened. Within a two-month period, we lost nearly $100,000 in annual funding. That really hurt! Now I felt that I was in way over my head. Many people told me to quit, but I couldn't leave the organization without getting them back to a financially stable position. I made a decision; I made a choice!

I decided to draw a line in the sand, step across it, and never look back. The choice I made was to leave the organization in much better shape than when I came on board. My goal, my vision, was to have six figures in unrestricted income at the end of any given month. We averaged approximately $14,000 per month, and now I had drawn the line in the sand and set my goal at a minimum of $100,000. This was late in 2001, and I set a deadline of December 30, 2002, to reach this bold goal.

Every morning, I sit in my hot tub and meditate. I visualize how I want that day and the rest of my future to be. For the next 14 months, as I sat in my hot tub, I said to myself, "Six figures in unrestricted cash by December 30, 2002." I would not leave this important goal to chance, so in addition to visualization, I also took action. I wrote grant proposals, letters to businesses requesting their support, and then I wrote more grant proposals. On December 30, 2002, I got the report from our office manager and found that we had a little more than $114,000. I had drawn a line in the sand, and I accomplished my goal!

My Friend Mike (Continued)

I told you about my friend, Mike Garcia, about how he and his mother were held hostage by her abusive ex-husband, and the tragic end that left his mother dead.

After Mike's mother was murdered, he made a choice to quit school. He chose to attract very bad people and bring them into his life. Some of these people were relatives, and others were criminals and drug addicts. Mike started breaking into houses, stealing guns, and carrying a gun. The Law of Attraction had given Mike just what he wanted—a life of drugs, thieving, and lying. He was literally living hand to mouth on the streets and was homeless.

The good news is that Mike got caught, arrested, and placed in the Platte Valley Juvenile Facility. That may not sound like good news, but it was. Once Mike was caught, he could no longer hurt people or victimize them. The streets of Greeley, Colorado were safer and so was he. He is very lucky that something more tragic didn't happen.

Mike's grandmother called me and told me he was in jail. After more than six court appearances, Mike was sentenced to two years probation and 64 hours of community service. We helped Mike set up community service hours both at the Boys and Girls Club and with IDEA WILD. Mike has completed his community service and is enrolled at Centennial High School, an alternative school program. Mike has been skiing with me and is doing well, but he has some new challenges in his life. Now he must choose to either stay in school or enter the Job Corps, which is run by the Bureau of Reclamation. He initially thought that he would like to be trained as a welder. His grandmother has really been pushing him to go into the Job Corps so he can get more structure and discipline in his life. I feel a little differently and think that, if he wants to have the greatest number of options in two to three years, he should complete high school and get back into competitive sports. Mike is one of the most gifted athletes I have ever known, and I have coached national champions in both tennis and soccer. Mike would make an excellent coach or counselor, but the choice will have to be his.

Something new has been added to this story. Mike left his grandmother's home one week after our avalanche accident and moved in with June and me. Mike attended the Rotary Youth Leadership Award camp for high school students and was chosen as a Junior Counselor for Young RYLA, a leadership camp for 8th graders. At that camp, Mike told his story, on stage, in front of 120 campers and 30 staff. There was not a dry eye in the room. He closed his presentation with a song that has a lot of meaning for him, *My Wish,* by Rascal Flatts.

Mike continues to get A's and received the STAR student award from his school. We are so proud of him and his positive progress and he is a true leader in his school. He has a passport and has begun to travel internationally. He has his sights on going to college. As my good friend John Goddard would say, "This story is to be continued."

*"I hope the days come easy and the moments pass slow,
and each road leads you where you want to go,
and if you're faced with a choice and you have to choose,
I hope you choose the one that means the most to you."*

∞ *My Wish* **by Rascal Flatts**

Getting It Done!

• Make a vow to always wear your seatbelt when you are in a car.

• What are some of the choices you have made? List the good ones and the bad ones. Go back and review them in your mind and make mental changes of how you could have made a better choice.

Chapter 5

Mentors: The Power of Association

"All who have acquired enduring riches have done it with two outstretched hands. One reaching upward to receive help, the other reaching down to aid those still climbing."
∞ **Napoleon Hill**

The Choice Is Yours

You do not achieve success, or go down the wrong road, without the influence of others. Your friends can take you down a good road or a bad road, but the choice will always be yours. No one can make you do something that you know is wrong, unhealthy, or illegal without your approval.

Bob Dow—The Power of Association

Robert "Bob" Dow was the editor of a newspaper in Jacksonville, Florida and was the uncle of my best friend, Joe Perry. When I was about 12-years-old, Bob started taking Joe and me out on archaeological digs with him. He taught us how to conduct excavations at an American Indian burial mound in a scientifically correct manner. At first, Joe and I were given areas to excavate in the "midden," which is basically the garbage dump for the old American Indian village. We found lots of shells, some broken points (arrow heads), and lots of pottery, mostly from broken pots. As our techniques got better, we were allowed to move our excavations into the burial mound. We helped out with the excavation of several burial sites, some with beautiful pots, some with shell necklaces and earrings. The site was eventually dated AD 85. WOW—almost 2,000 years old! All of the materials we uncovered were turned over to the Florida State Museum for proper cataloging and further study. We continued to be involved for many years and I have an interest in archaeology even today.

Bob took the time to teach something very unique to two young boys whom he cared about. He not only taught us about archaeology, he taught us many life skills as well. He taught us to be inquisitive, to ask lots of questions, to seek out the truth, and to find the answers to our questions. On the archaeological dig, we discovered much about the people and the culture from the remnants we excavated. We often found that their teeth had been worn down almost to the root—that had to be painful. We also found many had broken bones that had healed. "How did they break them?" we often asked. He talked of adventures and of visiting other sites in Mexico and South America. Bob also undoubtedly helped us increase our self-esteem and self-confidence, and he encouraged us to go to college and to seek out interesting careers.

Thanks to the experience I had with Bob Dow, when I was 15-years-old, I was invited on an archaeological expedition into the second largest desert in the world—the Arrub

Al-Khali in Saudi Arabia. WOW! I was a 15-year-old boy with nine adults traveling for four days, with no roads, in Land Rovers, across a vast desert expanse in search of a pre-Neolithic, or pre-agricultural site. We found the most beautiful projectile points (arrow heads) and flint sickle blades for cutting wild grain. We found Roman coins and bracelets and pottery at other areas as we traveled through the desert. We slept outside under the stars; there were so many stars!

As a direct result of Bob's influence, I studied biology and archaeology in college and pursued careers as an environmental scientist and teacher. I then became the executive director for a youth mentoring program in Colorado. Today I conduct leadership and motivational training for youth and try to inspire them, the way Bob Dow inspired me to seek out adventures and interesting and exciting things to study and do. I encourage every young person to write a "Life List" of all the things you want to do, see, and be and then take the necessary steps to make those dreams come true. I have traveled to more than 16 countries with my family, and we still seek out adventures and find interesting things to do and see. I owe many thanks to Bob for being such an important mentor in my life. I will never forget what he did for me. Everyone needs a Bob Dow in their life.

Antwone Fisher—The Power of Association Can Be Good and Bad

At the recommendation of friends, I watched the movie *Antwone Fisher* which is a true story about overcoming challenges and making something of your life! I also came

across a book review about Antwone Fisher's memoir called
Finding Fish, in a local high school newsletter. *Finding Fish*
was reviewed by Pam Downing, a media specialist at Rocky
Mountain High School, and as she put it, "It is a great read!"
Finding Fish is a great read for teens and adults alike who feel
angry or need a reason to hope. It is a painfully honest story
that illustrates the power of resilience and compassion in
the face of difficult challenges. This inspiring story is a great
reminder that life is what we choose to make it, no matter
what circumstances may come our way. It is also a powerful
reminder that peer associations can be both bad and good.
Antwone Fisher had every right to be angry as a young man.
He was born in jail and transferred between abusive foster
homes throughout his young life, and he ultimately chose
homelessness rather than living among the predators who
resided in the local inner city YMCA. After Fisher joined the
military as a very angry young man, he found that it was his
own rage that undermined his ability to move ahead in the
place he most wanted to succeed.

Fisher amazingly survived his enlistment because of his own
sense of resilience, but to move beyond survival, he needed
help. He found it in a compassionate and wise military man
who took the time to see the talent that was below the surface
of Fisher's pain. Fisher is an excellent writer. With caring and
dedication, Fisher's mentor helped him complete a successful
tour of duty, and he helped Fisher establish the inner strength
to go on to become a respected author and screenwriter.

Normally, I am not one to pick up a memoir, but I could
not stop reading this one. Fisher's narrative will hook you
immediately. He is brutally honest within beautifully written

passages. It's hard to believe he had no formal training as a writer, which makes this book all the more important for teens to read.

Finding Fish shows us that we can all succeed once we find that talent or purpose that is within each of us and we find the right people to associate with. With the help of a good friend and the courage to face the challenges that confronted him, Antwone Fisher proved that bitterness and anger do not have to interfere with attaining your dreams.

The book, *Finding Fish* and the movie, *Antwone Fisher* are about his true life story. Today, Antwone Fisher works in Hollywood as a director, screenwriter, author, and film producer. He used mentors and the positive power of association to prove that Dreams Do Come True! Way to go Fish!

Mentoring Mike

I told you about my friend Mike a few chapters ago. Mike and I have had a great time together. We started skiing, and within a very short time, Mike was skiing expert runs. He was very athletic and enjoyed going over jumps and skiing the bumps. We brought several of his friends and his brother, Stephan, skiing with us on a number of occasions. The Colorado Department of Public Health and the Environment received an opportunity for a new program called Mentors and Moguls that was sponsored by Christy Sports, and Mike was chosen for the photo shoot for the posters. Little did we know at the time that Nelson Carmichael, Olympic bronze medalist, would be skiing with us for that photo-shoot. Mike was 12-years-old at the time, and Carmichael gave Mike an unbelievable compliment when he told Mike, "You are a better skier at 12 than I was at the same age." You could see the wheels turn in Mike's head as he took in what Nelson told him. "You mean that I am a better skier than you were when you were 12?" he asked. "Yes," Nelson replied. "Keep at it—you could be very good someday."

Mike also had the great honor of meeting Herman Boone, the coach of the T.C. Williams High School Titans that the movie *Remember the Titans* was based on. Coach Boone once told Mike, "Never rest until your good becomes better and your better becomes best." Mike listened to Coach Boone and made dramatic improvement in his school grades, turning D's and F's into B's and C's. He was also the leading scorer of touchdowns in the seventh grade for all of the junior high school football teams in our city.

He had two groups that influenced him. The group that believed in Mike was a group of individuals, some of whom were very successful in both academics and athletics, and they offered to support Mike. The second group of people seemed to have a very negative impact on Mike, in my opinion, and steered him down a bad path.

I just can't stand to see young people who have so much talent waste their lives. There is a tremendous power of association, especially at a teen age. Unfortunately, Mike associated with a group that had a strong and powerful negative impact on his decisions. If you or anyone you know out there is in a similar situation, I only hope that you realize it, make a change, and get someone to help you before it's too late.

With all my heart I want all of you young people to succeed and reach those dreams that you have. All you have to do is believe and take that step in the right direction. The rest will happen, just trust me and believe!

"Never rest until your good becomes better, and your better become best."
∞ **Coach Herman Boone**

Getting It Done!

- Do you have people in your life who have affected you negatively because of your association with them? Break those ties today!

- Do you need a little inspiration to make positive changes in your life? Read about people that have had difficult times and made the correct choice of friends and mentors. Get inspired by them.

- Have you seen *Remember the Titans* and *Antwone Fisher*, or read *Finding Fish*? These stories are great examples of the positive power of association, so watch or read them on rainy days.

- Do you know someone who is going down the wrong road because of the people they hang with? If so, do what you can to help them realize the path they are taking is a dangerous path, even if it means losing that friendship.

- Hang with people that are moving in positive directions. Stay on the road to finding success through hope and happiness.

Chapter 6

Never, Never, Never Give Up: Keep On Keepin' On

"You are never a loser until you quit trying."
∞ **Mike Ditka**

If You Could Not Fail

What would you try if you could not fail? What sports would you participate in? What subjects would you study? What adventures would you go on? How would you leave your mark on the world and make it a better place?

Perseverance is the ability to continue toward a purpose in spite of difficulty, obstacles, or discouragement. We all face challenges and obstacles blocking our path. Some of us give up easily and just say, "It wasn't meant to be." But there are others who continue toward their goals without any thought of giving up. Why the difference? What can we learn from those who have achieved their goals through perseverance?

What other ways could we express the characteristic of perseverance?

A steady course of action:
Persistence • Tenacity • Pertinacity • Purpose
Dogged determination to hold on • Never, never, never giving up!

The following stories are about some people you have heard of and some you probably have not. They all have persevered to reach their goals—Bethany Hamilton, Thomas Edison, Steve Smith, Abraham Lincoln, Shaquille O'Neal, and Whoopi Goldberg. I hope that one of these stories will inspire you to greatness.

Bethany Hamilton: Uncommon Surfing through Perseverance

Bethany Hamilton has been surfing since before she could walk. Her mother and father were active surfers along with her two older brothers. She quickly learned how to surf on the beautiful beaches of Kauai, Hawaii. Bethany won the first surfing contest she entered, which marked the beginning of her amateur surfing career. In 2002, at the Volcom Puffer Fish Surfing Contest she placed first in the 14 and under girls' division, first in the 17 and under girls' division, and second in the 12 and under boys' division—yes, the boys' division! As of April 2002, Bethany was rated first in Open Women's, second in Open Girls', and second in Menehune Boys' divisions in the Kauai Surfing Federation.

At 13, Bethany had already achieved many of her dreams. She was an amateur surfing champion ranked eight in the world and was planning on pursuing a professional surfing career. In mid October 2003, she came in second at the National Scholastic Surfing Association Contest on the Big Island of Hawaii.

Things changed for Bethany on the morning of October 31, 2003. The day began as a typical, beautiful day in Hawaii. At Makua Beach, on the island of Kauai's north shore, the water was clear and the waves were relatively gentle. Just as she did most mornings, Bethany was surfing with her best friend, Alana Blanchard, and several other surfers.

Tragedy struck Bethany hard and fast that morning. At about 7:30 a.m., a shark about 14 feet long emerged from the water below Bethany and took a 17-inch-wide bite out of her orange, white, and blue surfboard. It also bit off Bethany's left arm just below the shoulder.

Bethany has recovered and is back in the water surfing and winning. Is her dream of becoming a professional surfer gone forever? I don't think so! She has incredible courage, a positive attitude about her life, and a strong spiritual belief. Bethany's perseverance is best described by a poster that the Foundation for a Better Life sends out to schools across the country. The poster is of Bethany standing on the beach holding her surfboard with a giant shark bite taken out of the board. She only has one arm. The posters says, Me quit? Never! You see, the shark may have swum off with Bethany's arm, but it didn't swim off with her dreams.

We all must overcome challenges in our lives, and Bethany Hamilton is no exception. She has put years of hard work in reaching for her dreams and goals, and with more hard work, courage, dedication, and encouragement, I believe her dreams will come true. Follow her comeback story and send her an encouraging e-mail by contacting her at www.bethanyhamilton.com. Bethany Hamilton, a story of uncommon success and courage!

Thomas Edison: A Man Who Defined Perseverance

Thomas Edison invented and perfected the incandescent light bulb, and it's easy to forget about many of his other inventions that we use every day, such as wax paper, tinfoil, the phonograph, and the "Edison Effect Tube," the forerunner of the television. Without his inventions, modern life would not be what it is today.

When Edison started working in Menlo Park, he told George Beard, a noted physicist, that he was organizing a workshop to turn out a minor invention every 10 days and a big invention every six months. Edison was granted 1,093 patents for his inventions, that is, a patent for every 10 to 12 days of his adult life.

Today, we focus on Edison's triumphs, but you should be curious about what kept him going after seemingly endless failures that eventually led to great inventions. After a thousand, or several thousand, experiments that did not produce the result he was seeking, Edison, would just say, "Well, we're making progress. We now know a thousand ways it can't be done. We're that much closer to getting there." He knew the answer was out there, and he knew the more he tried and failed, the closer he was to it.

How can someone, "keep on keeping on" and persevere in the face of not dozens or hundreds, but thousands of setbacks, dead ends, and seemingly endless failures? Thomas Edison believed the answer was out there and that each experiment that didn't work was just getting him one step closer to his goal. He didn't give up because he believed in what he was doing.

Steve Smith: A Man Who Never Gave Up On His Dream

This story was told by Neil Armstrong, the first astronaut to step on the moon, at a Charles and Anne Lindbergh Foundation Award Banquet.

When Steve Smith was growing up he had a big dream. His parents kept pictures of rockets, spaceships, and space travel that he had drawn in elementary school. Steve always wanted to grow up and become an astronaut. He studied hard in school and after graduating from LeLand High School in 1977, he went to Stanford and earned a bachelor's degree in electrical engineering in 1981. He then earned a master's degree in electrical engineering in 1982. Smith was a good student, but that's not the important part of his story.

He went to NASA to take the astronaut candidate entrance test and failed. He was not allowed to retake the test for two years. He studied for two more years and went back to NASA to take the test again, and again he failed. To retake the test again, Smith knew he would have to wait two more years. Most of us would have not had the level of perseverance required to fail at something twice and commit six years to trying to conquer it again, but Steve Smith did. He had a dream and would not be denied. He went back to Stanford, and in 1987, he received a master's degree in business administration. He returned to NASA to take the test again for a third time and failed again. He studied for two more years and went back to NASA to take the test for the fourth time, eight years after he had started pursuing this goal. He failed again.

Smith went to NASA for a fifth time, 10 years after he had taken the first test. In 1992, his dream came true, and he was selected as an astronaut candidate by NASA and reported for training in August 1992.

Smith was one of many astronauts to work on the troubled Hubble Telescope. After the Hubble Telescope was repaired, they took a picture called the "Deep Field Photo"—a photo of the darkest spot in the universe that required a ten day time exposure to capture it. WOW! What a wonderful world it revealed—thousands and thousands of galaxies each with more than a billion stars.

"We can do anything we want to do if we stick to it long enough."
∞ **Helen Keller**

Abraham Lincoln: The 16th President

President Abraham Lincoln was the 16th President of the United States of America. Before becoming our 16th President, he lost four elections for political office. Through his love of politics and his perseverance he was able to guide the United States through the Civil War and issue the Emancipation Proclamation on January 1, 1863, which freed slaves in the Confederate States. The Emancipation Proclamation led to the adoption of the 13th Amendment to the Constitution, which abolished slavery throughout the United States.

Lincoln came from humble beginnings. He was born on February 12, 1809, and though Lincoln had no formal schooling, he loved to read. Lincoln had a passion for government and law, so he studied law informally and passed the Bar Examination in 1836.

He first ran for public office in the Illinois State Legislature election in 1832, but was defeated. He persevered and ran again in 1834. He served four consecutive terms in the State Legislature before practicing law full time. In 1846, he re-entered politics and was elected to U.S. House of Representatives. After losing his re-election, Lincoln practiced law until he ran for the U.S. Senate in 1854 and lost. Lincoln lost again in 1855 when he ran for a different Senate seat. However, he gained national recognition and was nominated to run for President in 1860.

Lincoln was elected president, but before he took the oath of office on March 4, 1861, several southern states seceded from the United States. He raised an army following the Confederate attack on Fort Sumter and fought to save the United States' union. Lincoln was re-elected in 1864 and oversaw the Confederate States surrender on April 9, 1865. He proposed a speedy reunion between the North and South States but was shot by John Wilkes Booth on April 14 at Ford's Theatre and died the morning of April 15, 1865 before he could see his dream realized.

Shaquille O'Neal

Shaquille O'Neal, also known as Shaq, is one of the most prominent professional basketball players in NBA history. Towering at more than 7 feet tall, he has shattered records and backboards from the moment he arrived in the big leagues.

Shaq has helped win three NBA championship titles for the Los Angeles Lakers, been honored as MVP in each of those championships, led the league in field goal percentage five times, and been named one of the 50 greatest players in NBA history. These are not small feats, given the competition in the world-class environment of the NBA. He went on to win a fourth NBA championship with the Miami Heat.

There is another accomplishment that he has achieved that is less well-known but extremely important to Shaq. When he was drafted to the professional league from Louisiana State University in his junior year, he made a promise to return to finish his degree. One might wonder why he would worry about graduating from college since he had such a lucrative career and did not appear to need a diploma to be more successful in life. But Shaq had made a commitment to his mother, his school, and himself. He likes to keep his promises, but it was not easy for him to fulfill this one. He attended nine summer school sessions and finally graduated in December of 2000 with a bachelor's degree in general studies and a minor in political science. Unfortunately, the ceremony in Louisiana was scheduled on a game night. In a clear demonstration of what was really important, Shaq got permission to miss the game, though at a financial cost to him, and walked through the line of students at his commencement to mark this important milestone in his life—a promise kept and statement made that life really is more than a game. Since then, Shaq has earned a master's degree while he was playing in Florida. Why would Shaq continue to further his education when he has become the best in the game and has more money than he will be able to spend in his lifetime? He truly values education and as he puts it, "Life is more than just a game."

Whoopi Goldberg: The Actress Persevered Through Hard Work

Whoopi Goldberg was born in New York City in 1955, as Caryn Johnson. She spent the first years of her life in a public housing project in Manhattan. Over the course of her turbulent early life, she survived poverty, drug addiction, single motherhood, and a stint on welfare, to become one of America's most beloved entertainers.

Goldberg also struggled with dyslexia and, as a result, dropped out of high school. "I knew I wasn't stupid, and I knew I wasn't dumb. My mother told me that. Everybody told me I wasn't stupid or dumb. If you read to me, I could tell you everything that you read. They didn't know what it was. They knew I wasn't lazy, but what was it?" She remembers of her struggle. When she became an adult, she finally found the reason for her reading struggles was dyslexia. As Goldberg once recounted, "I learned from a guy who was running a program, and he had written a sentence on a board. And I said to him, 'You know, I can't read that.' And he said, 'Why not?' And I said, 'Because it doesn't make any sense to me.' So he said, 'Well, whatever you see, write exactly what you see underneath.' And so, he brought me to letters by coordinating what I saw to something called an A, or a B, or a C, or a D, and that was pretty cool."

She said it still takes effort, but time and hard work has made it easier for her to read. Even though Whoopi still suffers from dyslexia and must read thousands of pages of script, she hasn't let this obstacle stop her from achieving her dreams of being an actress and comedian. Thank you Whoopi for not giving up. I love your work!

"Whether you think you can, or you can't, you're right!"
∽ **Henry Ford**

Getting It Done!

- What would you try if you could not fail, or if you chose to persevere through failure? What sports would you participate in? What adventures would you go on? What would you invent? Write down a list of 10 things you would do if you could not fail.

- Which story of perseverance inspired you the most? Are there any other stories that inspire you to continue even when times get tough? Write down catchy titles to stories that inspire you and then share them with your friends. It's important to inspire others.

Chapter 7

Watch Your RAS: Programming Your Mind's Search Engine

"Whatever the mind...can conceive and believe, it can achieve."
∞ **W. Clement Stone**

I'm Too Busy to Focus

You are busy, very busy! How do you get everything done? How can you stay focused on your homework and your extracurricular activities and still stay in touch with your friends? And let's not forget trying to focus on your goals for the future—no way, no time!

Learning how to focus and get something done, whether it's getting good grades, gaining great athletic achievement, mastering a musical performance or artistic productions, winning competitive debates, or simply helping others, is the key for success in life. Let's talk about techniques for staying focused in the short term (day, week, or month), as well as learning the secret to staying focused in the long term, that is, staying focused in life. I believe that long-term focus is the most important component in seeking a lifelong path to success, so let's start there.

The Reticular Activation System—RAS

What makes us jump out of bed when we hear our cell phone ring but sleep through just about anything else, including constant pounding on the door by your parents to get you out of bed and on to school? It's the reticular activating system, or RAS, the part of our brain that constantly prompts us to take notice of what is relevant. What the RAS tells us is relevant, we focus on. What we focus on, we will reinforce. The RAS filters relevant from irrelevant information and only sends on to the brain the relevant stuff—the stuff that needs our attention or that we have determined by conditioning is important to us at the time.

Let me give you two quick examples. Has your family recently purchased a different kind or color of car? Did you notice shortly after that you began noticing all of the cars on the road of that same type or color? There is really no difference in the number of certain types or colors of cars on the road. The difference is that now your RAS has decided that recognizing similar cars is important and allows that information through, where before your RAS may have considered the same information to be irrelevant, blocking it from your conscious thoughts. Maybe you noticed the same thing with a particular style of clothing or an item such as a type of cell phone. Have you ever experienced that? Weird, isn't it?

The RAS sits at the base of your brain and helps filter out unimportant information the same way an Internet "search engine" does. So, why not program or direct your own personal "search engine," your RAS, to seek out and find the information that you need, whether it has to do with school, sports, extracurricular activities, or your future?

RAS Programming Instructions

Your RAS will work day and night 24/7 if it knows what you have decided is important in your life. To program your RAS for maximum efficiency and speed, you need the following: 1) know what you want, 2) a clear vision of the desired outcome, 3) some action toward your goals, 4) people who can help you reach these goals, and 5) the passion and desire to never give up.

Goals and Dreams: Your Road Map to the Future—So, the first step to programming your RAS is to know what you want and where you are going in life. You must have a list of what you want in life. We talked about this earlier in "Chapter 2—Show the World: Dreams Do Come True." John Goddard has shown us the power of creating a "My Life List." Once you have your "My Life List," and it is written down, then your RAS is already working to get you what you want. Go back and look at your "My Life List," and add to it if you have some new dreams and goals.

Vision—The clearer the vision you have of your dreams and goals, the better the chances of them coming true. Clarity is what you want. You need to be able to close your eyes and see the positive outcomes; see yourself achieving your dreams.

Visual imagery is taught to athletes but not to students in elementary, junior high, high school, or even college. Yet, we know it is one of the most powerful tools for achieving great success in athletics. Every Olympic champion has visualized themselves winning their event and standing on the podium, watching their country's flag being raised while the national anthem plays.

Cut out a picture of what you want to achieve and place it somewhere you will see it daily. It could be on your refrigerator, bathroom mirror, or even on your bedroom ceiling. A vision board is another great way to collect and display your dreams and goals.

Get emotional and feel what it will feel like when you achieve your goals. Anchoring your goals with a strong emotional connection is a sure way to make the attraction stronger.

"Vision is the art of seeing things invisible."
⚭ **Jonathan Swift**

Personal Initiative: Take Action—You have dreams and goals, and you have a crystal clear picture in your mind of you achieving those goals. You are well on your way toward achieving them, especially if you take action to move in the direction of those goals. Maybe you don't know what you should do. Let's take an example.

Let's pretend one of your goals is to have a career in healthcare. Maybe you want to become a medical doctor or nurse. You're not sure what to do or how to take action toward achieving that goal. Why not call your doctor, the one who you or someone in your family has gone to, and ask them if you could visit with them to discuss options in the healthcare profession? You could ask them why they went into the field of medicine, what they did when they were your age to start down that path, what would they do differently, and what are the best and worst parts of their job. Look at an online college catalog to see what the requirements are to get into a specific program or school and which classes you will need to take. Take some action, any action, toward learning more about your goals.

Attracting People to Help: Mentors— No one has reached a high level of success in any field without the help of others. Once you know what you want and you have started taking action through your personal initiative, then the next step to success is seeking out or attracting the people who can help you achieve your goals. *Webster's Dictionary* defines a mentor as "a faithful and wise adviser." Mentors can help you reach your goals faster. For example, if we were going to cross the United States from the West Coast to the East Coast, from Seattle to Miami, the person with prior knowledge of the road closures and a road map will get there faster. It's as simple as that. Mentors have more life experience and the knowledge that goes along with it; they can give you a "road map" to reaching your goals and dreams.

You have heard of six degrees of separation, the theory that anyone in the world can be connected to any other person through a sequence of acquaintances that has no more than five people in between. You know we are all much closer to people whom we need or want to meet, people who can help us down the road to success. Sometimes these people might be teachers, school counselors, coaches, relatives, friends of the family or members of your church. They can also be people you have only become acquainted with recently or someone who someone else knows. Keep an open mind and stay tuned in to opportunities to meet new people.

"Our minds become magnetized with the dominating thoughts we hold in our minds, and these magnets attract to us the forces, the people, the circumstances of life which harmonize with the nature of our dominating thoughts."
∽ **Napoleon Hill**

Never, Never, Never Give Up: Perseverance—In 1999, the Women's World Cup Soccer Tournament was being played in the United States. The U.S. team was one of the best teams in the world and was expected to do well in the tournament. Both of my daughters play soccer and wanted to see some of the World Cup, so as a family we purchased tickets to the semifinals and championship game months in advance. Our hopes were that the U.S. team would be in the finals.

As the time neared for us to travel to California for the games, we started searching for airline tickets from Denver to San Diego. I came home one afternoon and June had had it. She was upset. She said, "That's it. There are no tickets to California. I've tried everything to get us tickets. Different airlines, different days, and different times—nothing works. I've even tried three different travel agencies. You find us tickets."

I thought about Thomas Edison and how he tried things more than a thousand times before he reached his goal. I said, "We know at least three ways that won't work." She looked at me with that fierce, exasperated look that only a spouse can give you, she thought for a moment about what I said and then started laughing.

You see, I had told her just two days before about Thomas Edison's story of perseverance and how he tried thousands of times before he succeeded. She decided she would try again, and ended up, on the next call, getting us great tickets to San Diego for the days we wanted.

As a result of her perseverance, we were part of the largest crowd to ever watch a women's sporting event. There were 92,000 people watching as the U.S. Women's Soccer Team beat China in the finals of the World Cup Soccer Tournament. It was a dream come true for our daughters. It pays to persevere! And it can be fun!

> *"Most people give up just when they're about to achieve success. They quit on the one-yard-line. They give up at the last minute of the game, one foot from a winning touchdown."*
> ∞ **Ross Perot**

Multitasking: Does It Really Work?

Our house phone rang and it was for our youngest daughter, Logan. I asked the caller, a friend of Logan's whom we had known for many years, how she was doing while I walked the phone to the den where Logan was doing some homework on the computer. As I approached the computer desk, I noticed that Logan was on her cell phone, had several popup instant messages on the screen, was doing some research on the Internet, and was typing a paper. I was mad, to put it mildly. I walked up and told her to immediately hang up the phone, close the instant messenger, and concentrate on her homework. Logan asked the person to whom she was talking on her cell phone to hold on for a moment, she covered the mouth piece, turned to me, and said something to me that caught me really off guard. She said, "Dad, I'm a straight-A student. When my grades drop, we can have this discussion." I was stopped in my tracks. I didn't know what to say. I handed the phone to her, told her the call was for her, and then I walked away.

She was right. She was a straight-A student, always got her homework done on time, and it was of high quality. She was taking a number of Advance Placement classes and was well on her way to an outstanding academic record in high school. How could she do it? How could she multitask like that and still do quality work? I wondered what the quality of her work would be if she focused more on one task at a time.

Your generation has been dubbed "Generation M" by the Kaiser Family Foundation. The "M" stands for media multitaskers. Why? Because today, 82% of students are online by the seventh grade and boy, do you love the computer! You can listen to the radio, a CD, or iPod, play games, watch movies, e-mail, instant message, text message, "Google," and make pages on MySpace or Facebook, all while trying to do your homework. WOW!

Are students today more capable of multitasking than my generation was? I listen to music while doing some typing, and I truly believe it doesn't impact the quality of my work. But I know that if I am interrupted by the phone while writing, or if I switch back and forth between writing and e-mails, I am not as productive. Everyone is different, but generally, too many distractions can be detrimental to the quality of your work.

Many studies show that when people do lots of things at once they tend to do a worse job on all tasks than if they had focused on just one thing at a time. So when you multitask as you study, you're less likely to absorb and retain the information you need to do well on a test or an essay. So how do we stay focused on our school work?

Do you think multitasking is a useful skill? Think again! There is a ton of literature that shows that when people try to perform two or more tasks at the same time or alternate rapidly between them, e.g. instant messaging, e-mail, homework, etc., the errors increase and it takes far longer to complete your tasks than if you focused independently on them.

David E. Meyer, Director of the Brain, Cognition and Action Laboratory at the University of Michigan tells it like it is. "If a teenager is trying to have a conversation on an e-mail chat line while doing algebra, she'll suffer a decrease in efficiency, compared to if she just thought about algebra until she was done. People think otherwise, but it's a myth. With such complicated tasks you will never, ever be able to overcome the inherent limitations in the brain for processing information during multitasking. It just can't be. The toll in terms of slowdown is extremely large—amazingly so."

Now, for the good news: "Generation M" students tend to be extraordinarily good at finding and manipulating information, and are especially skilled at analyzing visual data and images, according to Claudia Koonz of Duke University. Many of you are brilliant and have a commanding use of media in your schoolwork. Way to go! However, please be cautious. Teachers and college professors are starting to notice a significant decrease in the ability of their students to write clear and focused narratives. Your writing skills are paramount to your long term success, so stay focused when you are writing.

Staying Focused in School

Staying focused on schoolwork requires six key steps, including: 1) Clearly defining your goals, 2) Planning ahead, 3) Breaking it down into small tasks, 4) Eliminating distractions, 5) Creating positive habits and routines, and 6) Rewarding yourself. Let's take a closer look at each of these critical steps.

Clearly Defined Goals—The starting point of staying focused is to clearly define your goals, assignments, and deadlines for your schoolwork, your job, and extracurricular activities. Goals are simply dreams with a deadline, so make sure you have clearly defined goals when things need to be completed and what will be required to complete the tasks. Do it for everything! Break all your deadlines into clearly defined goals for everything, even things such as your workout schedule, practice time for athletics and music, and art projects. Once you have goals with a deadline, it is much easier to plan for their timely execution.

Plan Ahead—If you don't have a day planner or PDA to write down all your deadlines then get one. You must have a central organized planner to write down all your appointments, commitments, and due dates for assignments, and then prioritize them. Once you have a schedule of upcoming events and they are prioritized, then you can better plan how to get everything done on time with high quality. Both of our daughters took Advanced Placement classes, participated in a number of service organizations or off campus charity activities, and played soccer. Planning ahead was critical for them and helped them get great grades and perform at their best.

Break it Down—Someone once asked, "How do you eat an elephant?" The reply was, "One bite at a time." Basically, you need to break larger projects, such as term papers and research projects, into small bite-size pieces. I have written thousands of pages for books, magazines, proposals, technical reports, and concept papers, and I have a technique that makes writing a 20-page term paper much easier. I have passed this trick on to both my daughters, and it has certainly worked for them. Here it is for everyone to use. Before you start any writing or research project, make a detailed outline of what you will be researching or writing about. Create headings and subheadings. As you research your topic, you might add some additional headings or combine a few depending on the information you find. Now it's time to write, and this part is easy. Simply fill in the information under the appropriate headings or subheadings. It's that simple. Generally, you will be writing two to five paragraphs under each heading. If you get stuck on one area, then simply move to a heading that you have more information on and work on that one. Give it a try, and I think you will be pleased with the outcome.

Eliminate Distractions—The best way not to give in to the temptation of media multitasking is to remove the option. You may need to go to the library or some other quiet place to read, study for exams, and work on projects if the temptation at home is too great. If you have a distracting home environment, then you need to plan ahead and find places where you can focus without distractions. Eliminate distractions, and your study time will decrease, the quality of your work will improve, and you will have more time for friends and leisure activities—a win-win-win situation for you, your grades, and your friends. Go do it!

Create Positive Habits and Routines—Good study habits and positive patterns are critical to shortening your study time and increasing your academic achievement. In determining if you have positive study habits and routines, I would simply ask, "What, when, where, and how do you study?" Your answer to these questions will give me a great insight into your study habits.

What should you study first? If you have a big assignment due tomorrow, then the priority of that task may take precedence over other assignments. You will want to tackle your most difficult and pressing tasks when you are the sharpest. Do not leave them for late in the evening when you are tired.

When do you study? Most of us have times of the day when we are at our best. Some people work best in the morning, and others, in the evening. The middle of the afternoon has always been the most difficult time for me to read, as I have a tendency to get very sleepy, so I try to do more active things during that time of the day. I am very productive and creative in the mornings, so I get up early and get my writing and critical thinking done early in the day. The evening is not my most productive or creative time of the day.

Where and how do you study? Reading textbooks and novels for school was always difficult for me to do at a table, so I almost always did that sort of task in a comfortable chair or on the couch. You will need to determine what works best for you. For instance, if every time you lie down on the couch or bed to read, you fall asleep, then that simply will not work for you. Go to a coffee shop or the library and stay sitting up. Math almost always needs to be done at a table, while writing usually needs to be done at a computer desk. Wherever you're working, make sure you have adequate lighting.

Reward Yourself—When you have completed a large task, reward yourself. It might mean you take time to snack on your favorite, tasty flavor of ice cream, call or e-mail a friend, or simply get outside to enjoy a walk or sunset.

Getting It Done!

In summary, here's a quick checklist of things that can help you stay focused on both your short-term assignments and activities and on your long-term goals in life:

- DO program your RAS.
- DO set deadlines.
- DO keep a schedule or calendar of tests, activities, and due dates.
- DO find a quiet place to study with all the materials you need.
- DO give it your best and stay organized.

Chapter 8

Leadership Is Not Just For Adults

"We're here for a reason. I believe a bit of the reason is to throw little torches out to lead people through the dark."
∞ **Whoopi Goldberg**

Lead With a Positive Attitude

A positive attitude is going to be one of your greatest leadership assets. Develop it, use it freely, and it will serve you well. We all know people who are fun to be around and lighten up the day. They always look on the bright side of things. They always are looking for something good in every setback. I love these people!

There are others who are a true pain to be around. They are always complaining and always have an excuse for their sub-par performance or under achievement. I have found that such excuses are usually false and nothing but lies. These "negative types" will bring you down and encourage you to settle for less than your best. I dislike these people intensely. Distance yourself from them!

I have always had a positive outlook on life, but since I was buried alive in an avalanche and was forced to come to terms with my own mortality, my attitude has become more positive than ever. I have been given another chance to live; why waste my life on negativity? I make a choice every day to have a positive attitude. You, too, can choose to have a negative attitude or a positive attitude. It's your choice. I choose a positive attitude and so should you!

If there was ever a time for high-quality leadership, that time is now! Just about everything we have been taught about leadership no longer applies to today's corporate or organizational world (let alone our political world). In fact, the principles usually taught by traditional leadership trainers are preventing us from being effective leaders today. Just about every popular notion about leadership turns out to be a myth rather than reflective of how "real-life leaders" function.

Leadership is not just for adults and we need your help now! Why aren't there more leaders? Why are people very reluctant to assume the "leadership role?" One possible explanation is because they are fearful or ignorant of what leadership truly means.

Leadership Myths and Realities

Lloyd Thomas is my friend and fellow Rotarian. He has more than 30 years experience as a life coach and licensed psychologist, and he dedicates a week of his own time each summer to the Rotary Youth Leadership Awards camps. I have the great pleasure of spending a week each summer with Lloyd, as we try to help approximately 120 middle school students develop the skills to become the leaders of tomorrow. Lloyd cares deeply about our nation's youth and is concerned by the myths of leadership that they often believe. Here are some old myths and current realities about today's leadership.

MYTH #1: Leaders are a small band of special people endowed with the ability to understand the mysteries of "leadership."
REALITY: Leadership can be learned and everyone plays a leadership role at some time in life. Effective leadership is everyone's business.

MYTH #2: Through personal power and control, leaders manage to maintain a "tight ship" so that their followers "toe the line," and the organization runs like clockwork.
REALITY: Contemporary leaders channel personal power and sound decision-making authority to their followers. They challenge the process of how "things have always been done." They shake up the status quo with new ideas, new methods, and sometimes, a totally new vision and purpose to attain desired results.

MYTH #3: Today's leaders are renegades who destroy "tried and true" ways of conducting business by attracting rebellious followers and engaging in courageous actions.
REALITY: Leaders are not defiant for defiance sake. They challenge the existing reality out of a deep faith in the ability of others to adapt, grow, learn, and realize their unique human potential.

MYTH #4: Leaders must succeed in the short term. They focus on quarterly or annual reports, identify current trends, and react to the immediate "marketplace."
REALITY: Genuinely effective leaders focus on the long-term purposes and goals to be attained in the future. They are future-oriented and ask themselves, "Does what I choose to do today support the creation of our collective fulfillment and desired outcomes?"

MYTH #5: Visionary leaders have some special "psychic powers" to know what is going to happen in the future, and they accurately predict it.
REALITY: It is important for leaders to have a vision of the desired outcome, but anyone can dream and learn ways to make their dreams a reality. A leader's vision may not come from "original thought." Leaders might adopt their vision from someone else or come to realize it over time based on what best expresses their values.

MYTH #6: The more you control others by incentive, power, manipulation, coercion, or intimidation, the better followers will perform.
REALITY: Genuine leaders know that the more they control, the less likely they will be trusted, and the less likely others will excel. They serve and support the people they lead.

MYTH #7: It is lonely at the top because leaders must remain cool and aloof toward those they lead. And no one but a select few knows about the "strategic plan" the leader has in mind.

REALITY: Leaders' deeds and actions are far more important than a strategic plan or their words, no matter how practical, inspirational, or enthusiastically expressed. Credibility and consistency of action are the most critical determinants of whether a leader will be followed over time.

MYTH #8: Leadership is a "position," and the position is superior to any other position within the organization.
REALITY: Leadership is a process of relating. It involves the application of personal and interpersonal skills and abilities whether they are within a position of leadership or not.

Whether you are a student, teacher, administrator, parent, friend, colleague, or role model, you can be a leader. So, you might as well set about honing your leadership skills according to the realities of today's world.

Your Leadership Traits

What are the character traits needed by leaders today? Some of the leaders of the largest U.S. companies are awaiting trial, on probation, or in jail. So, do we want to model our leadership traits after theirs? If we look at the papers today we might think that leaders must be deceitful, dishonest, or unethical. You know that is not right, but it does seem that way. Why? Are top business schools, which are often the pathway for our top corporate leaders, teaching these things? No, not at all. People who possess undesirable traits, whether they are your classmates, teachers, or in business, are not leaders. They most likely gained these negative character traits through learned behavior, either by watching someone or developing them on their own.

Let's take a look at some positive character traits of leaders.
Below is a list of character traits I have collected from
thousands of students at leadership retreats. If I knew
you very well and was giving you a recommendation for a
job you had applied for, which traits should I mention to
your potential employer? Circle all the traits that you truly
possess or that accurately describe you. Put an asterisk next
to no more than two or three characteristics that you need
to work on.

Do you:

Work hard	Give credit to the team
Follow through	Believe in serving others
Include others	Accept feedback
Challenge the team	Live passionately
Empower others	Believe in quality
Create excitement	Value others
Use "us" and "we"	Value yourself
Motivate others	Believe in yourself
Think on your feet	Work well with the team
Set high expectations	Take calculated risks
Believe in the team	Have a vision
Stay open-minded	Believe in the vision
Give feedback	Help others see the vision
Solve problems	Have personal integrity
Have a sense of humor	

Are you:

A "learner"	Charismatic
Courageous	Energized
Trustworthy	Poised
Non-judgmental	Loyal

Motivated	Fair
Caring	Responsible
Open-minded	Empathetic
Persistent	Organized
Inspiring	Sincere
A role model	Creative
Respectful	Humble
A good listener	Honest
Knowledgeable	Strong
A good teacher	Well-rounded

How do you stack up? Pick your top three to five character traits—the ones you feel are your strongest. Make sure when you are applying for a summer job or when you are completing your college applications and essays that you include these "key descriptive words." These words will separate you from the rest of the applicants and best describe you and what you are really like.

Very few of us aspire to be followers in everything we do. So, it might be useful to identify some characteristics of competent, ethical, and successful leaders to help you develop your leadership skills. Here are a few more words of wisdom from my friend Lloyd Thomas on the character traits of leaders.

Self-discipline—Any person who leads others needs to do so by example. If you expect those who follow you to be self-disciplined, you must be so yourself. Self-discipline is a willingness to do what needs to be done, even when you don't want to do it. Practice self-control to accomplish your objectives...step by step.

Fairness—Without a highly developed sense of justice, no leader will ever be respected by those whom she or he wishes to lead. If you treat everyone, including yourself, with fairness and respect, you will be emulated and receive the same in return from those who follow you.

Courage—When we confront common fears, such as rejection, others' opinions, and public speaking, for example, our fears usually diminish. Most of our fears are centered on non-dangerous, highly anticipated events or high-pressure situations. Courage to take reasonable risks is like stealing second base in a baseball game. You can't expect to succeed at it unless you risk taking your foot off of first base. No intelligent follower will follow a wimp. People who lack courage rarely risk anything.

High moral values—A study conducted by Harvard Business School a few years ago indicated that the primary characteristic needed most by top-level executives is integrity. The next one is a desire to serve the common good. Whatever happened to those character qualities? Dishonesty, undependability, lack of caring for others, greed, and an unwillingness to sacrifice oneself in the service of others may characterize some people, but certainly not long-term successful leaders.

Awareness and understanding—A competent leader must listen much more than talk. You were given two eyes, two ears, and one mouth—use them in those proportions. Only through observing and listening with the intention to understand does anyone become aware of another's perceptual world.

Assume full responsibility—The genuine leader assumes responsibility for the mistakes and shortcomings of his or her followers. Blaming or trying to shift responsibility to others always undercuts one's personal power and ability to take action to correct mistakes.

Attentiveness—Leaders must have a mastery of detail and be attentive to people and the organizations they lead. Efficient action requires detailed organization, strategic plans, and persistence.

Do whatever it takes—Leaders do more than they are paid to do. Leaders pursue their goal attainment with focus and a willingness to do "whatever it takes," within their moral and ethical standards, to reach their envisioned goals. Minimum effort attains only minimum results.

If you develop those personal character qualities yourself, you will be, by definition, a leader of character.

Ashley Shuyler is a Leader and Made a Change in the World

In the summer of 1996, Ashley went on a safari to Kenya and Tanzania. It was an experience that would change her life forever and prove wrong those who doubt that a teen can make a difference in the world.

While in Africa, she saw real poverty for the first time in her life and met numerous members of the Maasai tribe who touched her heart and soul. The African men and women she saw were always eager to please and help others, despite the hopelessness and desperation that surrounded them. They were willing to work as hard and as long as necessary to attain a better life, which, in Africa, takes a lot of work. Even for the relatively well paid, such as safari drivers, a pair of tennis shoes cost an entire month's salary. Seeing such an extreme level of poverty made Ashley realize how fortunate she was to be living in America. She saw that what we often take for granted in the United States is out of reach for so many Africans. Ashley believed education was the first tool that would help to better the lives of the impoverished. At that point, she decided to find a way to help those who might not otherwise be able to afford or even have access to educational opportunities.

Ashley believed that for those who live in countries where life is so bleak, surrounded every day by hunger, AIDS, illness, and desperation, that there is a vacuum so enormous that it is bound to be filled with something either hopeful or desperate and angry. She believed that we have an opportunity, and perhaps an obligation, for the future of our world to help provide education to these impoverished people. Ashley believed that education would empower these people and give them knowledge and information that they otherwise would not be able to get. And that is the key. Knowledge gives people the opportunity to make choices.

But what could Ashley Shuyler do? She was only a teen...In 2000, Ashley created AfricAid, a non-profit organization with a mission to help educate the people of Africa. Ashley is often asked why she started AfricAid. She recently wrote an essay describing how it all began. Here is an excerpt from her website that helps answer that question:

"As we drove away from the Nairobi airport, I looked at the world around me through the van window. Everything I saw seemed completely gray, without any variance in color, only in shade. I couldn't tell if this dullness was due to the sun's disappearance behind a cloud or if it was just the natural color of things. It was a gray of dirtiness. A gray of devastation. A gray of hunger. The people I saw seemed to know no life other than gray."

"As we stopped momentarily at an intersection, we rolled down our windows for ventilation. The hands poured in. The hands grabbed at us, poked at us, pleaded with us to buy the trinkets that they held. In the instant of my shock, I caught sight of a lone pair of eyes amidst the sea of hands."

"In the split-second that my hazel eyes were locked with those dark, brown eyes, I saw a profound look of emptiness that I had never seen before. I realized that the poverty that afflicted those eyes was worse than the lack of food or clothing that I had seen only moments before. No, those eyes reflected poverty so profound that it leaves a body hollow, with the resulting void destined to be filled by hopelessness."
"We soon left Nairobi, but that pair of eyes stayed with me. Their sadness and desperation left a permanent imprint on my soul. In my mind, the eyes continued to beckon to me to help them, to give them something to hope for. But I was not sure what it was that I could do."

"I found the answer in my own life, in my own school. I realized that the schooling I received every day opened up a world of almost limitless opportunities for me. I began to understand that knowledge has the capacity to inspire and enlighten; it empowers people, giving them the ability and opportunity to make informed decisions and the tools to take action. Only then can a better life—a life of hope—begin to take shape."

"So, I resolved to give that pair of eyes the opportunity to build that life, by providing the people I saw with an education that they might otherwise not have. After learning that many African girls have historically been denied the opportunity to receive an education beyond primary school, I started AfricAid, a non-profit organization that raises money and school supplies to benefit girls' education in Africa. I have seen these girls who, armed with an education, know what they can do to make their lives healthier, more meaningful, more complete. Energized and excited, they are sharing their new knowledge with family, with friends, with strangers. They are showing them that, through education, there is a life beyond despair. Thus, a ripple effect is created, starting with the knowledge of one person and touching many."

"It is in this way that I hope AfricAid will make its most lasting impact: by perpetuating an endowment of learning and hope that will fill the void that I saw in those two eyes. "
∞ **Ashley Shuyler, AfricAid founder**

So what have Ashley and the small group of dedicated teens on the AfricAid team accomplished? The year 2001 was a year of firsts for AfricAid. The first board meeting was held in April of 2001, the first fundraiser was in October, followed by the first donation of scholarships to The Girls' School in

Tanzania, the first school supply drive, the first newsletter, and the establishment of the organization's Web site, *www.africaid.com.*

In 2003, AfricAid continued its success with a successful fundraiser at the Denver Art Museum sponsored by the AfricAid Club, and an adventurous climb of Mt. Kilimanjaro in support of girls' education. Ashley also returned to Africa to the visit the Maasai Girls' Lutheran Secondary School and Maji ya Chai, another secondary school, and identified two new schools to support—The Oakland Girls' Secondary School and Losinoni Primary School.

2004 was a groundbreaking year with a return trip to Tanzania to participate in the construction of two new classrooms in the village of Losinoni and the completion of three additional classrooms in Usa River. Members of the organization also had an inspiring visit with the "AfricAid Scholars" at the Maasai Girls' Lutheran Secondary School, another successful fundraiser at the Denver Art Museum sponsored by the Colorado Academy AfricAid Club, and two successful benefit concerts in Utah. The first concert was sponsored by the Olympus High School AfricAid Club and featured Paul Cardall, and the second concert was organized by the Lone Peak High School AfricAid Club and featured Jon Schmidt. There were numerous other benefits spearheaded by youth across the country.

Obviously, teens can lead the way for adults and make a big difference in the world, if they want to.

A Final Note on Personal Leadership: A Mother's Advice

As you take various leadership roles in your life, you will often find that people will criticize you and make negative remarks about you. Don't worry! Just keep doing what you know is right, and you'll be just fine. In closing, I would like to leave you with some advice from a "mother" on your own personal leadership and what you need to do.

"People are often unreasonable, illogical, and self-centered;
Forgive them anyway.

If you are kind, people may accuse you of selfish, ulterior motives;
Be kind anyway.

If you are successful, you will win some false friends and some true enemies;
Succeed anyway.

If you are honest and frank, people may cheat you;
Be honest and frank anyway.

What you spend years building, someone could destroy overnight;
Build anyway.

If you find serenity and happiness, they may be jealous;
Be happy anyway.

The good you do today, people will often forget tomorrow;
Do good anyway."

*"Give the world the best you have, and it may never be enough;
Give the world the best you've got anyway."*
∞ **Mother Teresa**

Getting It Done!

- Know the myths and realities of leadership. Don't get fooled into believing that you cannot be, or become, a leader.

- Everyone is a leader at times. Everyone can improve their leadership skills through practice. Get busy practicing!

- List the leadership traits that you have. Make sure you put them on your college application letters and on job resumes.

- Most important, always be a leader of character!

- What do you think? Has AfricAid been worth all the time and effort that Ashley Shuyler put into it to get it started? After all, AfricAid is a tiny, tiny effort in a vast continent that has some of the most crushing poverty in the world. Has it made any real difference?

Chapter 9

Making a Difference: You're Only a Teen, What Difference Can You Make?

"I believe in karma; what you give is what you get returned."
∞ **Savage Garden,** *Affirmation* **(lyrics)**

You're Only a Teen, What Difference Could You Make?

How can you, a teenager, possibly make a difference in the world? Chances are you can't even vote yet. Money is hard to come by, and there are so many things you need and want. You don't have a high paying job, so you can't even donate money to a cause you believe in. You could donate your time to a worthy cause if you had some room in your schedule, but between school, sports, clubs, jobs, and of course, your social life, you don't have much free time at all, if any—and if you did, you would use it to catch up on sleep, right? You should want to make a difference any way you can because helping others will give you a sense of contributing to the world around you. It makes you feel that you can make positive changes in your environment and in people's lives, both those around you and others you may not even know. The uncertainty that often accompanies the teen perspective on the future becomes less ominous if you feel as though you are working toward improving the world around you. Your feelings of personal worth and self-esteem will come from within you, as opposed to coming from your peers. Performing acts of kindness and contributing gives you the feeling that good things happen in this world, and if you ascribe to the philosophy of Karma, you know that what goes around comes around. If you do good things, then good things will come back to you. It provides you with a feeling of well-being.

OK—Let's just say for a minute that you did have some money to contribute to a worthy cause and you also had some time. How could you make a difference? What cause would you turn your efforts toward and which friends would be willing to help you? Would you help out at the humane society, help save the rain forests, help the homeless, or read to children at an elementary school? Or, would you try to raise money to help change the lives of children on a different continent half way around the world?

"We must be the change we want to see in the world."
    ∞ **Mahatma Gandhi**

A Boy Making a Difference—The Starfish Story

A man was jogging down a beach one morning. The sun had been up for approximately two hours and it was starting to get hot. The tide was receding and all along the beach were thousands and thousands of starfish. Stranded at high tide the starfish were all going to die on the beach, as the sun rose higher by the minute. The seagulls had spotted the opportunity for an easy morning breakfast and were starting to swoop down on the helpless starfish.

As the man ran down the beach he noticed a young boy in the distance walking back and forth between the high tide mark and the water. As he got closer to the boy he observed that the boy was picking up starfish and throwing them back into the water. The man slowed his jog to a walk and approached the young boy.

The man stopped and asked the young boy what he was doing. The boy replied, "The tide is going out and these starfish are going to die, so I am helping by putting them back in the water." The man commented to the boy, "There are thousands maybe even a million starfish on this beach. Your efforts cannot make a difference." The young boy picked up another starfish from the beach, walked to the water's edge tossed it into the ocean and turned to the man and said, "It made a difference to that one."

This is the power of making a difference!

Ana Dodson—A Teen Leading the Way and Making a Difference

I met Ana when she attended the 2005 Young Rotary Youth Leadership Awards. I was giving a presentation on how to make your dreams come true—how to set goals, take action, find people to help, and never give up. I was telling the story of Ashley Shuyler, a young lady who, at the age of 15, started her own non-profit organization (AfricAid) to help educate Maasai girls in Tanzania. Ana raised her hand and quietly informed me that she knew Ashley. "How do you know Ashley," I asked. "She dated my brother," she replied, "and she inspired me to start my own non-profit."

Ana was an orphan in Peru when she was adopted by the Dodson family of Golden, Colorado. On a trip back to Peru to visit the place she had grown up, Ana became passionate about helping other orphans who had not been as lucky as her. She was concerned about the health and well-being of these children, so she took personal initiative and started Peruvian Hearts at 12-years-old! Peruvian Hearts is a non-profit organization, and its goal is to help provide education and enrichment opportunities for Peruvian children living in orphanages. The organization helps children by giving the additional resources needed to provide an environment that promotes and nurtures them physically, emotionally, spiritually, and educationally.

Ana's personal initiative and dedication to Peruvian Hearts has won her numerous awards. She won the Gloria Barron Young Hero Award and the Prudential Spirit of Community Award. Ana received the Spirit of Community

Award for being one of the top 10 youth volunteers in the United States. The recognition came with a cash award, which Ana used to start a scholarship fund for Peruvian girls in orphanages to further their education. She named the scholarship, "Maria's Gift," in honor of her biological mother, who never learned to read or write. Here are just a few of the things that Ana and Peruvian Hearts are doing to make a difference:

Vitamin Project—The Vitamin Project has made a significant difference in the quality of life for the orphaned children in Anta Cusco, Peru. One multiple vitamin a day can make the difference between malnutrition and good health for young children. Young people all over the country collect vitamins for the children in Anta Cusco. As a result, they have been able to supply the 16 girls at the orphanage and an additional 80 children who are fed daily at the Comidor Infantile with better health. Malnutrition is a big problem in this part of the world, and making a difference can be as simple as a daily vitamin. Your help can make a difference!

Good Health for All Project—Peruvian Hearts has arranged eye, dental, and medical exams for all of the children living at the orphanage. Last year, Evergreen dentist, Dr. George Kachidurain, worked on the 16 girls' teeth. He examined, X-rayed, treated 82 fillings, several extractions, and provided fluoride treatment for all. Imagine all that for just $550!

HEARTSTRONG—Peruvian Hearts has embarked on a new fundraising project. The idea was developed by Danny Dobson. Peruvian Hearts is purchasing wristbands embossed with the word "HEARTSTRONG," along with the symbol of a heart. They will say "Peruvian Hearts" on the inside and are available in a variety of colors and styles. They will be sending them out to Peruvian Hearts "Street Team" members across the country to support fundraising drives in schools, churches, synagogues, and communities.

Want to get involved? Go to the Peruvian Hearts website, *www.peruvianhearts.org*, and get involved. They have something for everyone. They have a Kids' Page and Teachers' Page with lessons and an area to inspire you to help out by starting a Peruvian Hearts Club at your school. Go ahead and make a difference!

"Never doubt that a small group of thoughtful, committed citizens can change the world; indeed, it's the only thing that ever has."
∞ **Margaret Mead**

Youth for Biodiversity

IDEA WILD is a non-profit organization founded by Wally Van Sickle. Wally is a wildlife biologist by profession and has a true passion for helping researchers around the world who are studying and protecting the biodiversity "hot spots" of our planet. He believes, as many others do, that our future depends on the understanding and preservation of these critical habitats. So, Wally raises money and gives small grants averaging approximately $750 to researchers around the planet. I had the privilege to be involved in one of his grants that empowered high school students to make a difference in the world. It's called "Youth for Biodiversity."

IDEA WILD's Youth for Biodiversity program seeks to nurture and empower young environmental leaders and philanthropists. IDEA WILD recognizes that tomorrow's leaders surround us today. However, these future leaders often lack the opportunity to engage in projects that foster community compassion while positively impacting local and international conservation efforts. The need for this kind of opportunity is urgent. Youth are not celebrated, nor are they perceived as agents of change by most people. Furthermore, we live in an ever-expanding nation where the populous competes for limited natural resources. This is a critical concern since this competition for natural resources inevitably impacts biodiversity conservation in our own backyard. Understanding and caring about biodiversity begins early in life, through education and experiential training. We hope our schools set priorities to explain the inter-relationships between all species, as well as model the importance of protecting those relationships.

However, educators cannot inspire on-the-ground environmental protection unless students participate in planning, advocating, and managing conservation projects. Furthermore, by empowering youth with the financial resources that would make these conservation projects a reality, they begin to understand the power of philanthropy and the importance of functioning as an agent of change. Lastly, by recognizing youth as community organizers and advocates, supporting their ideas, and celebrating their achievements, we help improve their self-confidence, vision, and character.

IDEA WILD recruits student leaders from middle and high schools that have an interest in biodiversity conservation. Students raise money to help support IDEA WILD projects. Here is one example of how students from Fort Collins made a difference. The students were able to take advantage of an opportunity arranged by Nature's Own, a retail store located in downtown Fort Collins. Roy Young, owner of Nature's Own, annually opens the doors of the store to a private Christmas shopping event called "Nature Goes Wild" wherein 100% of the store's proceeds from sales that day are donated to the Youth for Biodiversity program. The students in the program encouraged their parents, family, and friends to do all of their Christmas shopping that evening and raised a total of $3,035, which was matched nearly 10 to 1 by the Bohemian Foundation, giving the program a total revenue of $28,035. WOW!

The student group eventually funded a total of 48 projects in 18 countries ranging from Madagascar to Costa Rica, and even Indonesia. The project funded in Indonesia afforded binoculars and a global positioning system, or GPS, to researchers there. This equipment was used to discover a new bird species. Pretty cool stuff, all funded by teens trying to make a difference in the world. What other research did the group's funding help make possible?

- Sea Turtles, Barbados

- Andean Bears, Venezuela

- Scarlet Macaws, Costa Rica

- Bat Conservation, Madagascar

- Palawan Tree Shrews, Philippines

To learn more about IDEA WILD and how you can get involved in the Youth for Biodiversity program, visit their Web site at *www.ideawild.org.*

How Can You Get Involved in Making a Difference?

There are many ways to make a difference in your community and in the world. More opportunities exist today to help than ever before in every community. You can do it on your own like Ashley Shuyler did, or you can join in with other like-minded teens wanting to help by joining an existing service organization. These include, but are not limited to Boy Scouts, Girl Scouts, 4-H, FAA, church groups, and many school based service organizations. Rotary International and Kiwanis International sponsor the two largest school-based organizations providing both community and international service opportunities. The Rotary-sponsored high school program is Interact, and their college-based service organization is Rotaract. The Kiwanis-sponsored high school program is Key Club, and the college-based program is called Circle K. These clubs have been a big part of my life. I was a member of Interact at Wolfson High School. At St. John's River Junior College I was president of Circle K, and was recently the president of the Fort Collins Rotary After Work Club.

Interact—"Interact" is Rotary International's service club for young people ages 14 to 18. Interact clubs are sponsored by individual Rotary clubs, which provide support and guidance, but Interact clubs are self-governing and self-supporting. The membership base can be drawn from the student body of a single school or from two or more schools in the same community. The Interact Club of Fort Collins is made up of members from three area high schools. As one of the most significant and fastest-growing programs of Rotary service, with more than 8,600 Interact clubs in some 110 countries and geographical areas, Interact has become a worldwide phenomenon.

Interact gives young people an opportunity to participate in fun, meaningful service projects. Interact clubs perform several projects a year, with one servicing the community and the other furthering international understanding and goodwill. Through projects, Interact members develop a network of friendships with local and overseas clubs, develop leadership skills, and learn the value of hard work. You can learn more about Interact at *www.rotary.org/programs/interact.*

Rotaract—"Rotaract" is a Rotary-sponsored service club for young men and women ages 18 to 30. Rotaract clubs are usually community-based or university-based and are sponsored by a local Rotary club, making them true "partners in service" and key members of the Rotary family. Through the Rotaract program, young adults not only augment their knowledge and skills, but they also address the physical and social needs of their communities while promoting international understanding and peace through a framework of friendship and service. You can learn more about Rotaract at *www.rotary.org/programs/rotaract/information/about.html.*

Key Club—Key Club was started in 1925 and today is the oldest and one of the largest service programs for high school students in the world. What makes Key Club so successful is the fact that it is a student-led organization that teaches leadership through serving others. Members of the Kiwanis International family, Key Club members build themselves as they build their schools and communities.

Today, Key Club exists on almost 5,000 high school campuses, primarily in the United States and Canada. Growth efforts, however, have taken the Key Club experience internationally to the Caribbean nations, Central and South America, and most recently, to Asia and Australia.

Check out the Oakland High School Key Club in California, which is the biggest and oldest community service club at Oakland High. It has been around for 73 years! Past projects include the Coastal Clean Up, the Berkeley Soup Kitchen, Share Northern California, Daffodil Days, and much, much more. You can learn more about Key Club at www.keyclub. org/keyclub.

Circle K—Circle K is a co-educational service, leadership development, and friendship-building organization that is organized and sponsored by a Kiwanis club on a college or university campus. You can learn more about Circle K at *www.circlek.org/circlek.*

Getting It Done!

- How do you want to make a difference in the world? Start small with something in your school or community.

- What do you think are important issues that require attention in your school, community, and the world?

- Do you think one act of kindness can make a difference in someone's life? What can you do today to help someone?

Chapter 10

For Parents Only

"Having children is what life is all about."
∞ **Lawrence W. Boon**

A Question That Changed My Life

It was a beautiful fall day in Colorado, what we Coloradoans call an "Indian Summer." But instead of being outside enjoying the beautiful weather, I was busy working on a technical report to meet a deadline for one of my clients. They had me working more than 40 hours a week, so there I was, typing furiously on my home computer, working away on that beautiful Colorado morning.

Our oldest daughter, Denali, was four-years-old at the time. She walked into the office and watched as I worked away. I noticed her and said, "Hi. What's up?" She proceeded to drop a real bomb on me. She asked a question that was going to change my life and cause me to ask some real soul-searching questions. The question would set in motion a mid-life career change and would alter my life, my relationship with my wife, our financial plan, and many other facets of our life. The question was a very simple one for a four-year-old, but it had a gut-wrenching impact on me. The question was, *"Dad? Why don't you play with me anymore?"*

My mind went into immediate reasoning mode. The explanations started whirling through my head. I thought things like:

- I have an important job.
- The company that I work for has an important client whom we are helping with an environmental problem.
- The company has paid a lot of money for us to help them.
- Don't bother daddy because I'm very busy now.

However, nothing came out of my mouth. I could not come up with a reason that would make sense to my four-year-old daughter. So instead of defending my need to work, I simply asked, "What would you like to do?" She answered, "How about helping me catch grasshoppers in the garden." June and I had offered a bounty of one cent per grasshopper that was removed from our vegetable garden. We thought it would be an interesting option to pesticides and provide a unique opportunity for her to earn some extra money.

I said, "OK, let's go." I shut down the computer and caught grasshoppers, played Frisbee, played with the dogs, played a variety of games, had ice cream, and enjoyed the remainder of the day.

That night, after tucking Denali into bed, I went back to the computer and worked until the early morning. The next morning we went to the Denver Zoo and had another marvelous day. I wondered why I wasn't doing this more often. Family is what life is all about, right? That Sunday night, after putting her to bed again, I went back to work to have the client's report done by the Monday deadline.

On Monday at work, I delivered the technical report to the project manager's office, but there was no project manager there. I questioned his whereabouts and was informed that he was on a two-week vacation. I did not need to have the report done until he returned. Thanks a lot! I was sacrificing time with my family to meet a deadline that was essentially being self-imposed to meet my manager's convenience. Thinking back on the previous months and year, I had been consistently averaging more than 40 hours per week to meet many deadlines. Has something like this ever happened to you? It's happened to me more than I would like to admit.

The more I thought about it that week, the more I questioned why. June and I had made a conscious decision to try and meet our financial goals sooner by me taking this job. The salary increase had been close to 50 percent. Now it seemed that the increase in salary was taking a serious toll on our family and me. I contacted a very close friend, also named Dave, from college and asked if he could come to Colorado and spend the weekend with me. I had some serious soul-searching to do. He dropped what he was doing and came to my aid. He was a true friend back in college and still is to this day. We went to Rocky Mountain National Park and skied, watched wildlife, and talked about life. We laughed and we cried.

The following Monday, I handed in my two-week resignation letter. It floored everyone, but everyone was supportive and congratulated me for making such an important decision. Many of my co-workers said they would be walking out in the near future for similar reasons. None ever did. Surprising? Not really. June, of course, played a large part in helping me sort through what was most important. We spent many hours that weekend talking and soul-searching.

A Walk on the Beach—A Lesson in Parenting

I was walking down Fort Myers Beach for one of my morning inspirational walks while on a teaching and writing trip in Florida. I was staying in Jim and Ellie Newton's condo to complete the curriculum that I was writing for the Uncommon Friends Foundation.

I would get up early and start writing, and then around 10 a.m., I would take a break and walk two miles to the Fort Myers Beach Pier. This morning was like many others, calm sea and beautiful sky. I was approximately a half mile from the pier and noticed two families that had just arrived and were setting up for a day at the beach. Both couples looked to be in their late twenties or early thirties.

One couple was already digging out the buckets and shovels and beginning the task of building a sand castle with their son and daughter, who appeared to both be under 10 years of age. This couple was fully engaged in playing with their children; they were all having fun and surely developing memories that would last a lifetime.

The other couple had two boys who I guessed were about four- and six-years-old. As I got closer, I overheard the oldest boy ask his father if he would help them build a sand castle, and the father replied, "Go play by yourself and leave us alone." The father reached over and took a beer from the cooler. I looked at my watch and noticed that it was 10:05 a.m. The mother looked concerned but only said, "Listen to your father." This couple and their kids were also developing memories that would last a lifetime.

I stopped and pretended to look for shells to take in a little more of what was going on in front of me. There was a striking contrast between the engagement, or lack of it, with these two couples and their children. I could only think that there would be a very obvious difference in the outcome of the children's future self-confidence and self-esteem.

Then I heard a song come on one of the couples' radio. It was a country western song by Alabama entitled, *I'm In a Hurry to Get Things Done*. I thought about my life and the question that Denali asked me more than eighteen years ago and how I was in a hurry to get things done and had forgotten the most important job I had—raising healthy, happy, and productive children. I would like to be able to come back in a few years and check in with both families to see if the behavior I observed at the beach would have any positive or negative impact on the children's self-esteem and self-confidence.

"I'm in a hurry to get things done. I rush and rush until life's no fun."

≈ **Alabama, *I'm In a Hurry to Get Things Done***

A Question for Parents

How good a job have you done as a parent? Wow, tough question. It's the hardest job in the world, and there is no question about that. It's also a job that we have to learn through "on-the-job" training, from our past experiences growing up, through conversations with our friends, and through actual practice as we go. So, how have you done? Give yourself a grade like your kids get in school. Give yourself an A for excellent, B for good, C for average, D for poor and F for failing. How did you do?

My father once told me that having children was what life was all about. At the time, I wasn't married and had not had children yet, so I did not really grasp my father's words of wisdom. After having Denali and Logan, I came to believe that having children was what life was all about. But how was I going to do a good job at raising them and be a GREAT dad? This would be the hardest job I had ever had, one that I had little academic education and no training for. I did have a class in college on early childhood education and another on adolescent behavior. Believe me, these two classes did not adequately prepare me for the job of parenthood in the slightest. Nothing really can.

My parents, Rachael Creech Boon and Lawrence Winton Boon, were great role models as parents—the best. I guess the best I could do was copy their behavior. I received a few spankings as a child, all deserved, but nothing that left permanent scars, physical or emotional. My parents, both of them, would have received an A+.

Getting It Done

When was the last time you gave yourself a real reality check? Maybe it's past time for a little soul-searching. Our strongest and most important value was family, and we had allowed our desire for financial success to change our focus and priorities. By rearranging our priorities to make them more in line with our values, the Boon family became a more balanced family. We did give up short-term financial gains, but in the long term we greatly exceeded our financial goals and have attained many of the other riches of life that money cannot buy. Our lives changed, and we achieved more balance in our lives all because my innocent four-year-old daughter asked a very simple question—"Why don't you play with me anymore?" Thank you, Denali, for waking me up!

Place a letter grade next to each item below and give yourself four (4) points for an A for outstanding, three (3) points for a B for good, two (2) points for a C for average, only one (1) point for a D for poor and no points for an F for failing.

_____ Always being there for them

_____ Always being there when needed

_____ Always being positive and supportive

_____ Always being there for parent teacher nights, school meetings, games, recitals, club sports, and other events

_____ Spending more than 30 minutes each day in one-on-one meaningful conversation with your child

Total up your score and divide by five. That is your current grade. Now ask your kids to do the same. Don't be surprised if their score is different. Remember that their score is what the true reality is.

Your son or daughter has already completed a "My Life List." Ask them what that list is all about and have them share with you, if they are willing, some of the goals they listed. Encourage them and help them down that path to their success. That's your job as a parent! Make sure you give them an A+ effort. They deserve it!

About the Author

Some people are devoted to career while others are dedicated to leisure. Dave Boon's passion is to get teenagers excited about making good choices. Dave has won practically every civic and community award in any community where he resides. After raising two daughters and mentoring dozens, Dave found that he had a special purpose in life. This purpose goes beyond himself and even his own career...it was to assist teenagers on their path to happy and productive lives.

Dave has coached national champions in two different sports, spoken at a White House conference by invitation of the Vice President of the United States, and traveled the world's largest sand desert as a teen. He holds B.A. and M.S. degrees and has been a high school teacher, as well as a community college and university professor. Dave's innovative ideas and successful programs have been featured in *The New Yorker* and *Shape* magazines and highlighted by award winning Wall Street Journal reporters Bob Davis and David Wessel, in *Prosperity: The Coming 20 Year Boom and What It Means to You.*

These experiences were nothing compared with the lessons Mother Nature had in store. After an extraordinary event in 2007 (more about this in the pages that follow) Dave and his miracle survival story were featured on *Oprah, CNN, MSNBC, The Today Show* and in *USA Today.* Dave is convinced that he survived for a reason. Today his life work is focused on teaching goals, good choices and value based decisions in order to place everyone, but especially our youth on the road to hope and happiness.

Dave conducts leadership presentations throughout the United States and in Europe. Dave enjoys river rafting, snow skiing, tennis, traveling, and spending time with his family and friends. He lives in Fort Collins, Colorado with his wife June.

Tantalus — A king in classical mythology who, as punishment for having offended the gods, was tortured with everlasting thirst and hunger in Hades. He stood up to his chin in water, but each time he bent to quench his thirst, the water receded. There were boughs heavy with fruit over his head, but each time he tried to pluck them, the wind blew them out of reach. (Dictionary of Cultural Literacy)

Origin of the term "tantalizing."

My Wish